PRICE INTERDEPENDENCE AMONG EQUITY MARKETS IN THE ASIA-PACIFIC REGION

Price Interdependence Among Equity Markets in the Asia-Pacific Region
Focus on Australia and ASEAN

EDUARDO D. ROCA
School of Accounting, Banking and Finance
Faculty of Commerce and Management
Griffith University

Routledge
Taylor & Francis Group

LONDON AND NEW YORK

First published 2000 by Ashgate Publishing

Reissued 2018 by Routledge
2 Park Square, Milton Park, Abingdon, Oxon OX14 4RN
711 Third Avenue, New York, NY 10017, USA

Routledge is an imprint of the Taylor & Francis Group, an informa business

Copyright © Eduardo D. Roca 2000

All rights reserved. No part of this book may be reprinted or reproduced or utilised in any form or by any electronic, mechanical, or other means, now known or hereafter invented, including photocopying and recording, or in any information storage or retrieval system, without permission in writing from the publishers.

Notice:
Product or corporate names may be trademarks or registered trademarks, and are used only for identification and explanation without intent to infringe.

Publisher's Note
The publisher has gone to great lengths to ensure the quality of this reprint but points out that some imperfections in the original copies may be apparent.

Disclaimer
The publisher has made every effort to trace copyright holders and welcomes correspondence from those they have been unable to contact.

A Library of Congress record exists under LC control number: 99085932

ISBN 13: 978-1-138-70411-4 (hbk)
ISBN 13: 978-1-138-70410-7 (pbk)
ISBN 13: 978-1-315-20283-9 (ebk)

Contents

List of Figures   vi
List of Tables   vii
Preface   x
Acknowledgments   xii

1   Introduction   1

2   Equity Market Integration: Concept, Measurement and
    Existing Evidence   10

3   Statistical Framework   30

4   Price Interdependence between the Equity Markets of Australia
    and its Major Trading Partners   51

5   Price Interdependence among the ASEAN Equity Markets   78

6   Equity Market Price Interdependence between Australia and
    ASEAN   93

7   Investigation of Equity Markets Interdependence Allowing for
    Autoregressive Conditional Heteroskedasticity
    (ARCH) Effects   106

8   Summary of Results, Implications and Conclusion   141

Bibliography   148

List of Figures

1.1 Overview of methodology 4
1.2 Structure of the book 7
3.1 Econometric techniques and data used in the study 31
4.1 Average annual share in Australia's total trade: 1973–94 55
4.2 Australia's average annual trade balance with selected countries 56
4.3 Share of world capitalisation and rank, 1993 60
4.4 Market capitalisation, 1989–93 61
4.5 Turnover ratio and world ranking on turnover volume, 1993 62
4.6 Price-earnings ratio, 1993 64
4.7 Australia's response to a US shock 74
4.8 Australia's response to a UK shock 75
4.9 Hong Kong's response to an Australian shock 76
5.1 Response to a Malaysian shock 90
5.2 Philippine response to a Thailand and Singapore shock 91
5.3 Thailand response to a Philippine and Singapore shock 92
6.1 Australia's response to a Malaysia, Singapore and Thailand shock 104

List of Tables

2.1	Summary of major studies on equity market integration	20
4.1	Major institutional features of US, UK, Australian and selected Asian equity markets	65
4.2	Foreign shares listing in selected equity markets, 1989	66
4.3	Results of ADF and PP tests based on price levels for different subperiods Australia and its major trading partners	69
4.4	Results of ADF and PP tests based on price level difference for different subperiods Australia and its major trading partners	69
4.5	Results of likelihood ratio test Australia and its major trading partners	70
4.6	Computed trace values Australia and its major trading partners	70
4.7	Calculated F-statistics — Australia and its major trading partners	71
4.8	Forecast variance decomposition analyses Australia and its major trading partners	73
5.1	ASEAN regional trade	80
5.2	Characteristics of ASEAN markets, 1995	82
5.3	ASEAN equity markets capitalisation, 1988–95	83
5.4	ASEAN equity markets value of trade, 1988–95	84
5.5	Unit root test results — ASEAN	85
5.6	Likelihood ratio test on lags — ASEAN	86
5.7	Calculated F-statistics — ASEAN	87
5.8	Forecast variance decomposition analyses — ASEAN	88
6.1	Australia's trade with Southeast Asia, 1998	94
6.2	Australian merchandise exports to Southeast Asia, 1988–95	95
6.3	Australian merchandise imports from Southeast Asia, 1980–98	96

6.4 Level of Australian investment in ASEAN and other selected countries, 1988–95   97

6.5 Investment in Australia by ASEAN and other selected countries, 1988–95   98

6.6 Performance characteristics of Australia and ASEAN markets, 1995   98

6.7 Australia and ASEAN equity markets capitalisation, 1988–95   99

6.8 Australia and ASEAN equity markets value of trade, 1988–95   99

6.9 Unit root test results — Australia and ASEAN   101

6.10 Likelihood ratio test on lags — Australia and ASEAN   101

6.11 Computed trace values — Australia and ASEAN   102

6.12 Calculated F-statistics — Australia and ASEAN   103

6.13 Forecast variance decomposition analyses — Australia and ASEAN   103

7.1 Summary of stock market studies using ARCH methodology   122

7.2 Preliminary diagnostics for Australia and its major trading partners — period before deregulation   125

7.3 Conditional mean interaction between Australia and its trading partners — period before deregulation   126

7.4 Preliminary diagnostics for Australia and its major trading partners — period before crash   129

7.5 Conditional mean interaction between Australia and its trading partners — period before crash   130

7.6 Preliminary diagnostics for Australia and its major trading partners — period after crash   131

7.7 Conditional mean interaction between Australia and its trading partners — period after crash   132

7.8 Preliminary diagnostics for Australia, Taiwan and Korea — period after crash   133

7.9 Conditional mean interaction between Australia and Taiwan and Korea — period after crash   135

7.10 Summary of conditional mean interaction between the equity markets of Australia and its major trading partners   136

7.11 Preliminary diagnostics for ASEAN 136
7.12 Conditional mean interaction among the ASEAN 138
7.13 Conditional mean interaction between Australia and the
      ASEAN 140

Preface

This book undertakes a scholarly investigation of the issue of financial markets interdependence or integraton through the application of recently developed and powerful techniques in time series econometrics and through the use of a highly regarded database. The issue of financial interdependence is one that has theoretical, practical and policy significance, and yet it is far from being fully understood. This book investigates equity markets interdependence between Australia and its major trading partners, Australia and the Association of Southeast Asian Nations (ASEAN), and among the ASEAN markets. It analyses the extent and structure of equity market interdependence, both in the short-run and in the long-run within each group of markets taking into account important institutional developments in each country.

There are a large number of studies on equity market interdependence but most of these studies focus on the developed markets to the neglect of the markets that are the subject of the present study. Furthermore, most of these studies deal with either the short-term or long-term linkages between countries but rarely both. These studies are also beset with methodological, conceptual as well as interpretation problems. Hence, the existing evidence on equity market interdependence is generally mixed depending on the data, time period and methodology used. This book addresses this knowledge gap. Utilising weekly data over a 20-year period from Morgan Stanley Capital International, it applies the econometric techniques of cointegration, error-correction model, Granger-causality, forecast variance and impulse response and autoregressive conditional heteroskedasticity model analyses within a vector autoregression framework to investigate the structure of interaction between markets in the short-term and long-term.

The book is organised into eight chapters. The first chapter discusses the objectives and provides an overview of the methodology and overall results. The second chapter expounds on the concept of equity market integration and reviews the existing literature on this topic. The third chapter explains the different econometric techniques used in the book. Chapters four, five, six and seven present the empirical results for the three groups of markets which are analysed against the backdrop of the institutional features of each market that are relevant to equity market interaction. Chapter eight provides a summary of the overall results and the conclusion of the study.

The book will be useful to students of finance, particularly international finance, and investments at the third year undergraduate and postgraduate levels.

Acknowledgments

I am thankful to Professor W.F. Shepherd for encouraging me to write this book. He and Professor E.A. Selvanathan have provided me with guidance throughout the different stages of writing this book. I also thank Professor Dave Allen for his valuable comments and suggestions in relation to the whole book. I am also grateful to the School of Accounting, Banking and Finance of Griffith University for providing me with the much needed financial support to bring this book into completion. I also wish to thank Dr. Hai Yang Xu for the helpful comments and computer programming assistance that I have received from him. I extend my heartfelt thanks also to Ms Pam Cox for providing the typesetting and proofreading services. Finally, above all, I give praise to the Great Almighty for making this book project possible.

1 Introduction

Purpose of the Book

This book examines the issue of equity markets interdependence or integration. The issue of financial market integration is certainly one that is important from a theoretical, practical and policy perspective. Major models in economics, e.g., Mundell-Fleming (see Shepherd, 1994), and finance, e.g., portfolio diversification (see Markowitz, 1959; Lintner, 1965; Sharpe, 1964), depend on this issue. Based on portfolio diversification theory, it is important that investors are aware of the extent of financial integration between markets. If equity markets are less than fully integrated, the benefits of portfolio diversification exist. From a policy perspective, if equity market prices are found to be closely-linked, there is a danger that shocks in one market may spill over to other markets (the so-called "contagion effect" — see King and Wadhwani, 1990). Hence, this may require closer cooperation between the prudential and monetary regulators in the different markets if these effects are to be avoided or minimised.

Massive progress in information and communication processing technology and very substantial financial deregulation have occurred in financial markets over the last 20 years (Honeygold, 1989). Hence, it is claimed that financial markets have become integrated. The stock market crash of 1987 which was felt in markets worldwide is being cited as clear evidence of this interdependence between national financial markets (see, for instance, Hamao, et al., 1991, and King and Wadhwani, 1990). This claim is captured well by the Wall Street Journal of 9 November 1987 (as cited in Jeon and Von Furstenberg, 1990, p. 15):

> They (investors) were saying for a long time that the stock market was global. But no one really believed them until that day (October 19, 1987). Moreover, the crash may have laid to rest Americans' long-held notion that New York always led the pack among world stock markets. The old axiom 'When New York sneezes, Tokyo and London catch a cold', has become outdated. Now it changes to 'anyone can catch a cold from anyone'.

1

The issue of financial market integration in general, and equity market integration in particular, is, however, far from being settled in the literature. Investigations done on the issue have failed to reach a common conclusion.[1] The results of previous studies vary according to the data, methodology and theoretical models used. Furthermore, most of these studies have focused on the developed markets and very few have been undertaken for the emerging or developing markets such as those in the Asia-Pacific. This book therefore seeks to fill this knowledge gap. It investigates the extent and manner of equity market price interactions among the following groups of countries:

(a) Australia and its major trading partners (Japan, Hong Kong, Singapore, Korea, Taiwan, the US and the UK)
(b) the Association of Southeast Asian Nations or ASEAN (Malaysia, Singapore, Indonesia, Philippines and Thailand)
(c) Australia and ASEAN

For each group of equity markets, the book aims to answer the following questions:

(a) To what extent are prices between markets significantly linked, both in the short-term and in the long-term?
(b) Which markets lead and which ones lag?
(c) How fast and how long do interactions occur between these markets?

The Asia-Pacific region, on account of its glowing economic performance over the past 15 years, has attracted the attention of investors worldwide. However, recently, Asian countries have been engulfed in a financial crisis, which started as a currency crisis in Thailand in July 1997, and which has quickly spread to other countries, mainly Indonesia, Malaysia, Philippines, Singapore, Hong Kong, Korea and Japan. Stock markets in the region have plummeted severely as a result of the currency crisis. Financial observers have been surprised by the speed by which the crisis has spilled over the region and there are therefore claims that this situation is hard evidence that the Asia-Pacific financial markets have become integrated. However, very little is known about the linkages among the Asia-Pacific markets since the level of research in the area has focused on developed markets. This book addresses this gap by investigating the equity market linkages among the three groups of countries within the Asia-Pacific region. Each of these groups of countries has been characterised by increasing trade interaction and has experienced significant deregulation over the last 15 years. Hence, it is claimed that these markets have become integrated or interdependent. The results from the examination of these three cases therefore provide new evidence on equity market integration.

The book examines the price linkage of the Australian equity market with those of its main trading partners and those of ASEAN. It also investigates the price linkage among ASEAN equity markets. Australia's equity market relationship with its major trading partners and ASEAN has not been systematically explored. Australia's relationship with its major trading partners has changed over the years, with the bulk of Australia's trade shifting from the US and the UK towards the Asian countries. The Asian countries which are Australia's major trading partners are mainly the northeast Asian countries. Singapore is the only southeast Asian country that is a major trading partner. However, Australia's economic interaction with ASEAN has also been significant and there is a conscious push in Australia for a closer integration with the region. The ASEAN countries themselves as a group have started to become closely integrated economically, given some initiatives which have taken place among the groupings. Australia, its trading partners and the ASEAN countries have all undertaken substantial financial deregulation. This has liberalised and opened their financial markets to international investors. Thus, it may be expected that Australia's stock market may have become integrated with those in its major trading partners and in ASEAN. The ASEAN countries, likewise, may have become integrated given their increasing economic interaction. The few studies that exist on ASEAN financial market interdependence have examined the banking, money or bond markets but not the equity market. Thus, the results from the examination of each of these three case studies can provide fresh evidence on the issue of equity market integration.

Overview of the Book's Methodology

In order to achieve the objectives of this book, equity market interdependence is examined using the following recently developed and powerful techniques in time series econometrics (see Figure 1.1):

(a) cointegration and error correction model (ECM);
(b) Granger-causality;

(c) forecast variance decomposition and impulse-response function;
(d) autoregressive conditional heteroskedasticity (ARCH) model.

Cointegration is used to examine the long-term aspect of equity market interdependence while Granger-causality, forecast variance, impulse response and ARCH model-based analyses are utilised to investigate the short-term aspects of interdependence. These techniques are conducted within a vector autoregression (VAR) context — a nonstructural econometric modelling approach which best suits the study of stock market prices. A highly regarded database is used — the Morgan Stanley Capital International (MSCI) weekly indices covering the period 1975–95.

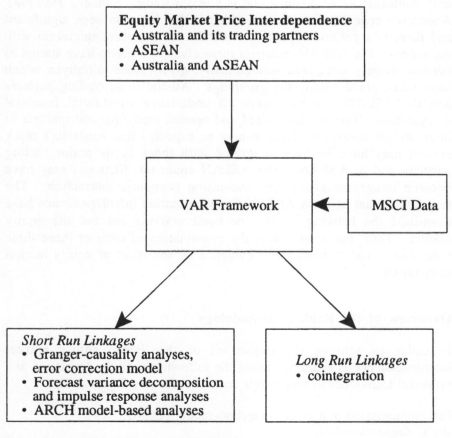

Figure 1.1 Overview of methodology

Through its use of advanced econometric techniques, the book provides more robust and comprehensive evidence on the issue of equity markets interdependence as it is able to overcome the major problems encountered by previous studies on equity market integration (Jeon and Von Furstenberg, 1990). Some problems pertain to the use of differencing in order to make variables stationary, the inability to simultaneously analyse short-term and long-term relationships among variables, and the use of noncomparable stock market data (see, for instance, Kwan, et al., 1996). The current book overcomes these problems through the use of recent advances in econometric time series analysis — cointegration analysis using the Johansen (1988) procedure, Granger-causality, impulse response, forecast variance and ARCH model-based analyses. Differencing achieves stationarity of data but important long-term relationships contained among levels of the variables are lost. Cointegration allows the determination of long-term relationships among nonstationary variables. Its associated error-correction model together with Granger-causality and variance decomposition and impulse response analyses, allow a more rigorous scrutiny of the short run linkages between the markets in terms of identifying the markets that lead or lag, and the speed and duration of interactions between markets. Previous studies on integration have either concentrated on the short-term or on the long-term, with most concentrating on the short-term.

The use of the Johansen (1988) method in conducting the cointegration test ensures that the results obtained from this book are more robust than those of previous studies. The advantages of this approach over other methods, e.g., Engle-Granger (1987) and Engle and Yoo (1987), are well-recognised in the literature. However, previous studies on equity market integration which have used cointegration have not used the Johansen approach (see, for instance, Kwan, et al., 1996). The robustness of the results from this book is further ensured with the use of ARCH model-based analysis. The use of this technique enables the analysis to capture the effects of time varying or conditional volatility in the interaction between markets. Conditional volatility is a feature of financial time series data that is well-recognised in the literature. However, many of the previous studies on equity market integration have neglected this (see for instance, McNelis, 1993; Jeon and Von Furstenberg, 1990; Cheung and Mak, 1992; etc.).

The use of the MSCI stock market indices is also another factor that contributes to the robustness of the results of the book. The MSCI indices are highly regarded among finance scholars and researchers for their comparability and avoidance of double counting. The book uses MSCI weekly data covering a 20-year period (1975–95). The use of weekly data avoids problems associated with daily data, e.g., "too much noise" (Bailey and Stulz, 1990) and day-of-the week effects, and monthly data, i.e., month-of-the year effects.

Structure of the Book

The book is organised into eight (8) chapters (see Figure 1.2). A brief description of each chapter is provided below:

Chapter 1 states the general and specific objectives of the research, presents an overview of the methodology, and establishes thoroughly the theoretical, practical and policy contributions of the book. It also discusses how the book is structured and provides a preview of the results of the book.

Chapter 2 discusses the concept and measurement of equity market integration and reviews the major literature on equity market integration. Here, the case for defining integration in terms of interdependence is established. The rationale is also provided for using non-structural time series techniques based on VAR.

Chapter 3 discusses in detail the econometric techniques used in the book: cointegration, error correction model, Granger-causality, and forecast variance and impulse response analyses. The detailed discussion of the ARCH methodology is, however, not done here but is undertaken in Chapter 7. The ARCH analysis is conducted in a separate chapter in order that its results can be compared to those obtained from the use of other techniques. The ARCH analysis is used to further examine the results obtained from the application of the other techniques.

Chapters 4, 5 and 6 report the results from the application of the techniques that were discussed in detail in Chapter 3. Chapter 4 discusses the results for Australia and its major trading partners; Chapter 5 the results for ASEAN; and Chapter 6 the results for Australia and ASEAN. Chapter 7, as already mentioned, discusses in detail the ARCH model-based methodology and reports the results of this methodology for the three groups of markets. The results obtained here are compared to those presented in Chapters 4, 5 and 6. Chapter 8 presents a summary of the results, discusses the implications of these results and then provides the conclusion of the book.

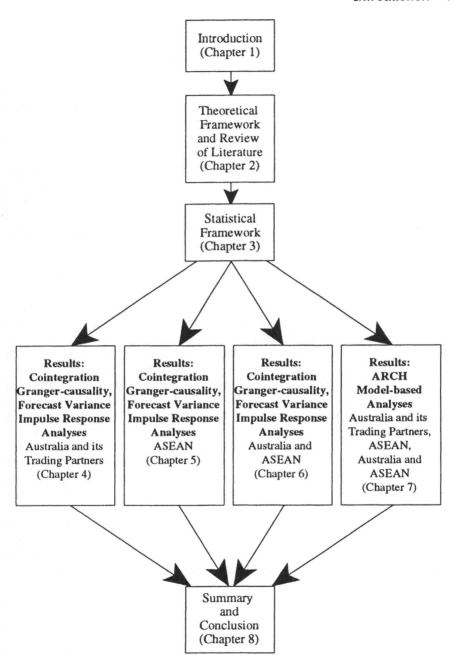

Figure 1.2 Structure of the book

Overview of the Book's Findings

For Australia and its major trading partners, the analysis is conducted over three sub-periods to take into account major structural breaks: before financial deregulation (1974–83); before the stock market crash (1984–87); and after the crash (1988–95). No cointegration was found in each of the three subperiods. This suggests that there is no significant long-term linkage between the equity markets of Australia and its major trading partners. The results of the Granger-causality, forecast variance and impulse response analyses and ARCH model-based analyses reveal that Australia is significantly linked to the US and the UK in the short-run and that the interaction occurs within a period of four weeks. These results therefore indicate there is "inefficiency" in the international transmission of news between Australia and the US and UK markets and that long-term Australian investors can make use of the equity markets of Australia's major trading partners as venues for portfolio diversification. Short-term Australian investors, however, cannot make use of the UK and the US for portfolio diversification.

In the case of the ASEAN equity markets, the analysis is undertaken during the period 1988–95. No cointegration is found. The markets in this group are not significantly related in the long-term. However, in the short-term, with the exception of Indonesia, all the ASEAN markets have significant linkages with each other, as revealed by the results from the Granger-causality, forecast variance decomposition and impulse response analyses. Malaysia is the most influential market while Singapore and Thailand are the markets with the most linkages with other markets. Indonesia is not linked at all with any other ASEAN market. Generally, each market responds to a shock from another market within a week, and the interaction continues, although at a much lower level, beyond two months. The ASEAN markets therefore offer diversification benefits to long-term investors within the ASEAN region.

Finally, in the case of Australia and ASEAN, the investigation is also conducted over the period 1988–95. The book finds that they are cointegrated and are therefore significantly linked in the long-term. In the short-term, the Granger-causality, forecast variance decomposition and impulse response analyses show that Australia is significantly influenced by Malaysia, Singapore and Thailand although this is not further supported by the ARCH-based analyses. Australia responds to a shock from these markets within a week and continues to do so until week 10. The Australian equity market is not significantly linked with those of the Philippines and Indonesia. The ASEAN markets therefore do not serve as good avenues for long-term portfolio diversification by

Australian investors but in the short-term, the Philippine and Indonesian markets do.

In conclusion, the book clearly shows that Australia has significant linkages with the US and ASEAN in the long-term and with the US, UK, Malaysia, Singapore and Thailand in the short-term. These results are in line with the results of previous studies. Australian financial regulators should therefore explore the possibility of coordinating their policies with those of the US, UK, Hong Kong, Malaysia, Singapore and Thailand. ASEAN markets are not significantly linked in the long-term but generally are in the short-term. Australian investors can derive diversification benefits from Australia's major trading partners (with the exception of the US and Singapore) in the long-term, from Indonesia and the Philippines in the short-term and from Japan, Taiwan and Korea in both the long-term and short-term. Long-term investors within ASEAN can reap diversification benefits from ASEAN markets. The results also show that there is inefficiency in the transmission of news within the markets studied and thus, this offers possible arbitrage opportunities for investors.

Note

1   For studies that claim that markets are integrated, see for instance, Agmon, 1972; Ripley, 1973; Hillard, 1979; Ibbotson, et al., 1982; Jaffe and Westerfield, 1985; Schollhammer and Sand, 1987; Wheatley, 1988; Hamao, et al., 1990; Espitia and Santamaria, 1994; among others. For those that claim the opposite, see, Grubel, 1968; Makridakis and Wheelwright, 1974; Adler and Dumas, 1983; Jorion and Schwartz, 1986; Levy and Lerman, 1988; Dwyer and Hafer, 1988; Jorion, 1989; Smith, et al., 1995; among others

2 Equity Market Integration: Concept, Measurement and Existing Evidence

Introduction

This chapter provides a theoretical discussion of the general issue of equity market integration. It also reviews the existing evidence on this issue based on the results of previous studies. The chapter is organised into five sections. The first section is the introduction. This is followed by two sections which discuss the concept and measurement of equity market integration. The fourth section reviews the existing studies on equity market integration while the last section provides the conclusion to the chapter together with a table summarising the major studies on equity market integration

Financial market integration is generally defined in terms of equality of asset prices which in turn require asset substitutability and capital mobility (Shepherd, 1994). In terms of equity market integration, this translates into equality of expected stock returns. Operationally, however, financial market integration is better defined in terms of market interdependence, following Kenen (1976). Equity market integration, in particular, has been studied in terms of (a) degree of price equality, (b) degree of price co-movement, (c) speed and duration of price co-movement, and (d) degree of barriers. Asset pricing models have generally been used in the existing literature to study these aspects but these models have been plagued with problems. Non-asset pricing models which utilised such techniques as correlation, cointegration, Granger-causality, variance and impulse response analyses have recently been used in studying (b) and (c). The existing evidence on equity market integration in general is inconclusive.

The Concept of Equity Market Integration

The present study is an investigation of financial market integration — particularly equity market integration. It is therefore fundamentally important that the concept of financial integration be understood thoroughly. This section seeks to fulfil this need.

Theoretically, the concept of financial market integration is based on the "law of one price". Financial markets are said to be integrated if assets of the same risk in different markets result in the same yield as measured in a common currency (Stulz, 1990). When yields happen to be different, the process of arbitrage is expected to bring these prices back into equality (Shepherd, 1994). In terms of equity market integration, this translates into equality of expected stock returns, which may be expressed mathematically as:

$$E\left(r_i\right) = E\left(r_j\right) + E\left(\Delta e\right)$$

where:

$E\left(r_i\right) =$ expected stock return in country i,

$E\left(r_j\right) =$ expected stock return in country j,

$E\left(\Delta e\right) =$ expected percentage change in the value of country j's currency in terms of country i's currency.

A further reflection on this definition reveals that this implies that assets are perfectly substitutable and/or that capital is perfectly mobile. Shepherd (1994) posits that perfect asset substitution implies the existence of uncovered interest rate parity while perfect capital mobility implies the existence of covered interest rate parity. Due to the existence of barriers to the exchange of financial assets, e.g., regulatory, informational, etc., then the forward premium does not necessarily coincide with the expected exchange rate change, and therefore perfect asset substitution does not necessarily equate to perfect capital mobility. Furthermore, uncovered interest rate parity may not even hold due to the presence of risk premia in foreign exchange markets due to such factors as default risk.

The difficulty of meeting these requirements in the real world necessitates a distinction between the theoretical and operational definition of financial market integration (Shepherd, 1994). Operationally, financial market integration is more usefully defined in terms of price interdependence between markets, following Kenen (1976). In Kenen's words, capital market integration refers to "the degree to which participants in any market are enabled and obliged to take notice of events occurring in other markets. They are enabled to do so when information about those events is supplied into the decision-making processes of recipients. They are obliged to do so when it is supplied in ways that invite them to use it in order to achieve their own objectives — to maximise income, wealth or satisfaction" (Kenen, 1976, p. 9).

Measurement of Equity Market Integration

Equity market integration has been studied through the examination of any one or a combination of the following attributes of financial market integration: (a) degree of price equality among markets, (b) degree of co-movement of prices, (c) degree of barriers, and (d) speed of price adjustment. Each of these attributes have been investigated in the literature in the following manner:

Degree of price equality International asset pricing or risk-return models have been used in measuring the degree of asset return equality among markets. The idea is that if risk-adjusted asset returns among markets are equal, then markets are integrated. Two major models have been used prominently: (a) the capital asset pricing model or CAPM, and (b) the arbitrage pricing theory or APT. The CAPM was originally developed by Markowitz (1959), Sharpe (1964) and Lintner (1965), and first extended into the international setting by Solnik (1974a). Several forms of the CAPM have been used ranging from the multiperiod version (Merton, 1973) to the consumption-based version (Wheatley, 1988). Numerous studies on equity market integration have used the CAPM (see, for instance, Agmon, 1972; Solnik, 1974b, 1974c; Stehle, 1977, Stulz, 1981; Jorion and Schwartz, 1986; Wheatley, 1988; among others). Results obtained from the use of the CAPM, however, have been criticised due to well-known problems associated with the model, i.e., non-testability (Roll, 1977) due to the impossibility of constructing a market index and the difficulties in meeting its assumptions, e.g., no imperfections among markets, quadratic utility function for investors, homogeneous expectations, etc. Because of these weaknesses of the CAPM, the APT has been used as an alternative by many studies on equity market linkages (see for instance, Gultekin, et al., 1989; Solnik, 1988; Korajczyk and Viallet, 1989; Darby, 1986). The APT was first developed by Ross (1976) and first extended into the international scene again by Solnik (1983). It avoids the use of the market index and only requires that investors have quadratic utility function. However, it requires that different sources of risk be identified. Unfortunately, these sources have not yet been definitely identified. This is therefore the main weakness of the APT. Furthermore, a fundamental criticism to the use of asset pricing models in testing equity market integration is that the test becomes a joint test of integration and the validity of the model. Interpretation of the results of such tests therefore becomes a problem. Markets may be actually integrated but the results may show segmentation simply because the asset pricing model used has failed to hold. Because of these problems, some researchers have avoided using asset pricing models in their investigation of equity market integration. Instead, they analyse the price of similar assets. For instance, Marr, et al. (1991) analysed the degree of integration among markets by comparing the price of the Euroequity component of a stock offering with the price of the domestic component. The problem with this approach, however, is that it is difficult to find assets of identical risks.

Co-movement of prices   Three approaches are usually used in measuring co-movement: (a) correlation, (b) cointegration, and (c) Granger-causality. If asset returns are correlated, then equity markets are interpreted to be integrated. Correlation has been used in several studies (see, for example, Grubel, 1968; Ripley, 1973; Adler and Dumas, 1983; Dwyer and Hafer, 1988; Bailey and Stulz, 1990; Cheung and Ho, 1991; among others). However, there has been a number of criticisms as to its validity. For instance, there is the possibility of obtaining spurious correlations among asset returns because equity markets are subject to many common factors, e.g., business cycles, international agreements, etc. Researchers have responded to this criticism by differencing the data so that correlations are calculated based on changes in asset returns rather than on level of asset returns. Such an approach, however, results in the loss of certain important properties which are associated with levels. Another criticism has centred on the stability of correlation matrices (Eun and Resnick, 1984) which makes it difficult to say with certainty whether the correlation coefficient that has been obtained is something that applies to the whole period or not. Finally, there is the basic criticism that correlation alone does not give any information as to whether there is a causal relationship among the markets, and if there is, what the direction of the causality is.

Cointegration and Granger-causality avoid some of the difficulties associated with correlations. Cointegration, first introduced by Engle and Granger (1987), avoids differencing of the data. It allows the determination of long-term relationships among markets which are derived from the levels of the data. Cointegration "has been regarded by many econometricians as the most important recent development in empirical modeling" (Charemza and Deadman, 1992, p. 116). It has been reliably used in equity market integration studies (see, for instance, Shafie, 1993; Arshanapalli and Doukas, 1993; Chan and Lai, 1993; To, et al., 1994; among others). Granger-causality (Granger, 1969) is able to detect the direction of interaction among markets. Some of the studies which have used this technique are those of Malliaris and Urrutia, 1992; Cheung and Mak, 1992; Smith, et al., 1993 and To, et al., 1994. Cointegration and Granger-causality analyses, however, require large amount of time series data.

Speed and duration of interaction As stated earlier, the faster the adjustment of prices to equality, the more integrated the market is. This attribute has been measured through the use of error correction models or ECM within cointegration and impulse response multipliers and variance decomposition analysis available in vector autoregression or VAR models (Sims, 1980; Eun and Shim, 1989; Espitia and Santamaria, 1994, etc.). The ECM shows the adjustment from the short-run to the long-run in the asset returns after a disturbance happens. The impulse response multiplier indicates the dynamic impact of one market on other markets over a certain period of time while the variance decomposition analysis shows the accumulated degree of impact for the whole period. VAR has the advantage of not requiring the use of asset pricing models and is easy to estimate. However, it requires extra care in selecting the lags to be used and in sequencing the variables. VAR is also criticised for being a theoretical and therefore not suited to testing hypotheses. As in the case of cointegration, VAR also depends on a large size of data.

Factors Affecting Equity Market Interdependence

The extent and structure of interdependence between equity market price can be due to the following factors:

Economic integration The more integrated the economies are, the more integrated equity markets are (Eun and Shim, 1989, etc.). It is well-established in the finance literature, based on the dividend discount model, that stock prices are affected by movements in dividends and the discount rate which are both affected by the level of economic activity. Thus, when economies are integrated, any disturbance in a particular economy not only affects its own stock market but also the stock markets in other economies. This has the effect of increasing price co-movement. This of course presupposes that markets are efficient vis-a-vis economic news (Fama and French, 1988; Fung and Lie, 1990; Fama, 1990).

Related to economic integration, Janakiramanan and Lamba (1997) argue that the market with the dominant economy in the world will cause its stock market price to drive prices in stock markets of other countries. This is because economic factors affecting the dominant country's economy and currency will have repercussion in the economies of other countries. This will then cause co-movement in the stock prices between countries, but the dominant market, of course, will have greater influence on the smaller markets. Thus, the US equity market is well-accepted in the literature as the dominant stock market whose price drives prices in other equity markets (Espitia and Santamaria, 1994).

Price co-movement between any two markets can also be the result of each of these two markets' reaction to another market, such as the US market. Espitia and Santamaria (1994) discovered that the interaction among the European equity markets was very much due to each market's interaction with the US market so that when the US market was not included in the analysis of the linkages between European markets, the results did not make any sense at all. Price co-movement between two markets can also be due to the reaction of one of the markets to the indirect effect of a third market. For instance, Eun and Shim (1989) found that the Australian market reacts to the US market on day 1 and then on day 2 reacts to the UK reaction to the US market.

Multiple-listing of stocks   Another factor that can contribute to co-movement of stock prices between countries is multiple stock listing. For instance, suppose a share is dually listed in both stock markets A and B. Shocks in stock market A can be transmitted to stock market B through this share. When there are many such shares, then the transmission from stock market A to stock market B becomes greater. In fact, in a study conducted by Gjerde and Saettem (1995), as cited in Janakiramanan and Lamba (1997), it was found that the Swiss stock market is affected substantially by other European markets because a large number of shares in the Swiss market are multiple-listed in other European markets. In the present study, however, this factor is controlled since the data used do not include multiple listed stocks.

Regulatory and information barriers   Regulatory and information barriers determine the degree and speed of capital mobility and portfolio readjustment in response to changes in asset returns and news from each market, hence, the higher the degree of barriers, the lower is the degree of equity markets integration. There have been attempts in the literature to take into account the presence of investment barriers in the testing of equity market integration through the use of asset-pricing models which have been constructed based on the assumption of the existence of investment barriers (Black, 1972 and 1974; Eun and Janakiramanan, 1986; Hietala, 1989). However, the use of these models require the measurement of the effectiveness of investment restrictions. This is difficult to do as investors find ways to evade explicit restrictions (Bonser-Neal, et al., 1990, p. 256; Campbell and Hamao, 1992, p. 43). Another way that has been used to indicate the degree of barriers is to look for evidence that cross-border transactions in financial assets are limited. A problem with this is that a limited volume of cross-border trading might be sufficient to bring asset prices into line across markets (Campbell and Hamao, 1992, p. 43).

Institutionalisation and securitisation   Institutionalisation promotes equity market integration as institutions are more willing to transfer funds overseas (Fabozzi and Modigliani, 1992). These institutions are more willing to venture overseas in search of diversification opportunities. Examples of these institutions are country and global funds, e.g., Korea Fund, Taiwan Fund, Templeton Funds, etc. Securitisation or the use of securities in raising funds encourages companies to cross list shares in different stock. This facilitates the process of international diversification as investors are able to tap shares listed in different exchanges, and thus, securitisation has the same effect as institutionalisation in promoting integration between equity markets (Honeygold, 1989).

Market contagion   King and Wadwhani (1990) theorise that prices between national stock markets can move together because of a contagion effect. Over reaction in one market can spill over to another market resulting in movement in prices which are not justified by market fundamentals. Investors in one market infer information from prices in other markets and hence, a "mistake" in one market can be transmitted to other markets. This situation, according to the authors is a kind of situation within a "non-revealing market equilibrium", and may be a credible explanation for the simultaneous fall in equity prices worldwide during the stock market crash of 1987. Previous research claim that "contagion is typically greater during periods of turbulence than during tranquil times, that it operates more on regional than on global lines, and that it usually runs from large countries to smaller ones" (Calvo and Reinhart, 1996 as cited in Goldstein, 1998, p. 17).

Present Evidence on Equity Market Integration

There exists an extensive number of studies on equity market integration. However, there is no agreement among these studies as to whether or not equity markets, in general, are integrated. Results generated by these studies vary according to the model, methodology, data, sample and time period used. As a compromise, it is concluded that equity markets are neither integrated nor segmented. The present study attempts to address this gap in the literature in its attempt to provide fresh evidence.

Studies on equity market integration have primarily examined the following issues:

(a) whether equity markets are integrated or segmented;
(b) whether the linkage between equity markets are stable or unstable;
(c) whether there are groupings among markets in terms of linkages;
(d) the manner of interaction among equity markets — which markets are influential, how one market affects another market, and the speed of interaction among markets.

As mentioned earlier, the results of these studies are mixed. Some have concluded that equity markets are integrated (see, for instance, Agmon, 1972; Ripley, 1973; Hillard, 1979; Ibbotson, et al., 1982; Jaffe and Westerfield, 1985; Schollhammer and Sand, 1987; Wheatley, 1988; Hamao, et al., 1990; Espitia and Santamaria, 1994; among others). Other studies reported that equity markets are segmented (see, for instance, Grubel, 1968; Makridakis and Wheelwright, 1974; Adler and Dumas, 1983; Jorion and Schwartz, 1986; Levy and Lerman, 1988; Dwyer and Hafer, 1988; Jorion, 1989; Smith, et al., 1995). With respect to the stability of equity market linkages, again, the results of previous studies are divergent. Some studies found equity market linkages to be stable (e.g., Panton, et al., 1976; Philippatos, et al., 1983; Goodhart, 1988; among others). Others claim that linkages among equity markets are unstable (see, for instance, Makridakis and Wheelwright, 1974; Maldonado and Saunders, 1981; Jorion, 1989; Roll, 1989a and 1989b).

A number of studies have examined the manner of interaction among equity markets in terms of the influence of one market over the other, the manner of response of markets to influences coming from other markets, and the speed by which shocks or volatility from one market are transmitted to other markets. There is overwhelming evidence that the US equity market is the most influential stock market in the world (see, for instance, Khoury, et al., 1987; Schollhammer and Sand, 1987; Fischer and Palasvirta, 1990; Espitia and Santamaria, 1994).

Considering that the Japanese equity market is the second largest in the world (in fact, in certain years in the past, it was the biggest), there is the expectation that it would at least exert significant influence on other markets, particularly in the Asia-Pacific. The results from previous studies do not provide a clear answer. Lee (1992), after analysing the relationship between the stock markets of Japan, Korea, Taiwan, Hong Kong and Singapore, using monthly data from January 1970 to December 1989, concluded that Japan is not an influential market. Becker, et al. (1990) and Jaffe and Westerfield (1985) reported that the Japanese equity market had only a small impact on the United States stock market during the period 1985–88. On the other hand, Jeon and Von Furstenberg (1990) and Hamao, et al. (1990) had found the Japanese market to be less interdependent with the US stock market since the crash of October 1987. To, et al. (1994), however, found the Japanese equity market to be influential on the Asian emerging markets.

With regard to the existence of leads and lags among markets, the overwhelming evidence is that the United States leads other markets, with the exception of such markets as Korea, Taiwan and Thailand (see, for instance, Khoury, et al., 1987; Eun and Shim, 1989; Fischer and Palasvirta, 1990). There are, however, some studies that reported no lead/lag relationships among markets (e.g., Granger and Morgenstern, 1970; Hillard, 1979).

On the issue of transmission of shocks between markets, the results of other previous studies have also been mixed with some reporting that the transmission process is efficient, i.e., occurring within a period of one to two days (see, Schollhammer and Sand, 1987; Khoury, et al., 1987) while other studies (e.g., Ng, et al., 1991) reported the process to be inefficient.

Some studies point to the existence of a linkage between certain groups of equity markets based on some unifying or common factor, such as close regional, economic, and geographical relationships. To, et al. (1994) found the following clusters: Japanese and Asian emerging markets, and the UK and African emerging markets. Hillard (1979) discovered a close association among intra-continental markets during the oil crisis of 1973 while Jorion (1989) reported a high degree of linkage among European continental markets. An Anglo-Saxon cluster was also reported by Jorion (1989).

The findings of previous studies on equity market linkages should, however, be taken with caution. First, most of these studies have been based on asset pricing models. Others have used correlations and other econometric techniques which are beset with certain shortcomings which the present study overcomes. Second, some of these studies, e.g., Koch and Koch (1993), Malliaris and Urrutia (1992), and Eun and Shim (1989), used daily equity market data or monthly data (e.g., McNelis, 1993). As emphatically pointed out by Bailey and Stulz (1990), the use of daily stock market data is problematic for two reasons: daily stock market data contain too much noise and portfolio investors make their portfolio readjustment on a horizon longer than a day, probably at least a week. Also, daily data is subject to the so-called "day of the week" effect while monthly data is subject to the month of the year effect. Lastly, these studies have also failed to dissect the distinction between the long-term and short-term aspects of financial market integration. The structure of integration has been hardly analysed in the existing literature.

Conclusion

Equity market integration is defined in the context of the law of one price, and is usually studied in terms of four attributes: (a) equality of asset prices, (b) price co-movement, (c) speed and duration of price movement and (d) degree of barriers. Factors such as economic integration, multiple listing of stocks, institutionalisation, securitisation and market contagion affect the extent of integration between different equity markets. The existing evidence on equity market integration is mixed, and existing studies have mostly focused on developed markets and are beset with different problems ranging from theory to methodology to data. This study investigates the issue of Australia–Asia equity market integration and focuses on attributes (b) and (c). Very few studies have been done on this area and most of these studies have either focused on the short-term or on the long-term. Most of them also suffer from problems with methodology and data. A summary of the major studies on equity market integration is presented in Table 2.1.

Table 2.1 Summary of major studies on equity market integration

Author(s) and Objective(s)	Type of Data and Period
• **Aggarwal and Soenen (1989)** Investigates the diversification gains to US investors of investing in the Asia-Pacific fixed-income and equity markets.	Weekly data for the US (S&P500), Japan (Nikkei Stock Average), Australia (All Ordinaries), Singapore–Malaysia (Straits Times), Hong Kong (Hang Seng), Philippines (Manila Mining) and Thailand (Bangkok Book Club) from 1981 to 1985; commercial bank deposit rates for 1981–85; foreign exchange rates.
• **Agmon (1972)** Examines the relationship between four stock markets.	Monthly stock market index data for the US (Fisher Arithmetic Index and Dow Jones), UK (Financial Times Ordinary Share and Economist/Extel Indicator), Germany (Frankfurter Allgemeine Zietung) and Japan (Tokyo Stock Exchange Price and Dow Jones Tokyo) for the period Jan. 1955 to Oct. 1966.
• **Akdogan (1995)** Conducts three studies to investigate equity market integration within Europe, and between the US and Europe.	Monthly stock market data obtained from the International Financial Statistics (IFS) published by the International Monetary Fund were used in all studies; for the first study: UK, Germany, France, Netherlands, Belgium, Denmark, Italy and Spain using data from 1978–92; for the second, study: Belgium, Denmark, France, Germany, Italy, Netherlands, Spain, UK, Australia, Norway, Sweden, and Switzerland with data from Jan. 1972 to Feb. 1992; and for the third study: European Union, European Free Trade Association, and Americas using the same data as the second study.
• **Arshanapalli and Doukas (1993)** Tests linkages and dynamic interactions among stock markets.	Daily data for New York (Dow Jones Industrial Average), Frankfurt (FAZ General Price), London (FTSE 100), Japan (Nikkei 225), and Paris (CAC General Price) from 1 Jan. 1980 to 31 May 1990.
• **Bailey and Stulz (1990)** Estimates benefits of diversifying into the Pacific Basin markets.	Daily, weekly and monthly stock market data for US (S&P 500), Australia (All Ordinaries), Hong Kong (Hang Seng), Japan (Nikkei Dow 225), Malaysia (Industrials and Commercials), Philippines (Manila Mining), Singapore (All-Share), South Korea (Composite), Taiwan (Weighted) and Thailand (Bangkok Book Club) from Jan. 1977 to Dec. 1985.

Methods	**Results**
Mean-variance and correlation analysis.	Low correlations between returns in the US and the Asia-Pacific markets (both fixed-income and equity) even after accounting for exchange rate changes, therefore, there are substantial benefits to US investors for diversifying into the Asia-Pacific markets.
Single-index market model version of the capital asset pricing model where the US index is used as the world market index.	US, UK, Germany comprise a "single multinational equity market"; high degree of relationship among the four markets; no significant lags in the response of non-US markets to changes in the US market.
Different formulations of the Capital Asset Pricing Model were used: single index, bifactor, market size-adjusted, regional and international.	Markets were segmented in the late 1970s but have become integrated in the 1980s.
Unit root and cointegration analyses	Increased degree of interdependence among stock markets after the crash of 1987 with the exception of the Nikkei index; US significantly affects the French, German and UK markets while the Japanese market has no links at all with the other markets.
Mean-variance and correlation analysis of returns (same day, lagged one day, weekly and monthly).	Substantial benefits arise for US investors if they diversify into the Pacific markets due to relatively low correlation between the US and Pacific Basin markets; correlation figures differ for daily, weekly and monthly data — the longer the time interval, the higher the correlation; random walk hypothesis is supported better by weekly and monthly data than by daily data.

Table 2.1 (continued)

Author(s) and Objective(s)	Type of Data and Period
• **Becker, et al. (1990)** Investigates the relation between the US equity market's previous day's closing price and Japan's stock market's present day's opening price as well as between Japan's previous day's closing price and the US' present day opening price.	Daily opening and closing data for the Nikkei Index, S&P 500, and yen/dollar exchange rate from 5 Oct. 1985 to 25 Dec. 1988.
• **Campbell and Hamao (1992)** Investigates the integration between the US and Japanese equity markets.	Value-weighted index of the New York Stock Exchange and the Tokyo Stock Exchange; 1-month Treasury bill yield and 20-year government bond yield for the US; and for Japan, the combined call money rate (Jan. 1971 to Nov. 1977) and the Gensaki rate (Dec. 1977 to March 1993) and a value-weighted index of yields on bonds with 9 to 10 years to maturity; period covered is from Jan. 1971 to March 1993.
• **Dwyer and Hafer (1988)** Examines the linkages among four major equity markets.	US, Germany, Japan and UK; daily stock market prices from July 1987 to Jan. 1988 and monthly stock market prices from 1957–87 broken down into 1957–73 and 1973–87 periods.
• **Errunza and Losq (1985)** Examines theoretically and empirically whether equity markets are integrated or segmented.	Monthly return data for heavily traded securities from Argentina, Brazil, Chile, Greece, India, Korea, Mexico, Thailand, Zimbabwe and the US for the period 1976–80.
• **Espitia and Santamaria (1994)** Examines the interdependence among markets and how changes are transmitted from one market to another.	Tokyo, New York, Frankfurt, London, Madrid, Milan and Paris; daily indices from Oct. 1987 to Sept. 1992.
• **Eun and Shim (1989)** Examines the international transmission of stock market movements.	Daily Morgan Stanley Capital International stock market indices for Australia, Canada, France, Germany, Hong Kong, Japan, Switzerland, UK and US covering the period 31 Dec. 1979 to 20 Dec. 1985.

Methods	Results
Correlation and regression analyses using OLS.	US previous day closing price has a high influence on Japan's present day opening price; however, the present day's opening price of the US is not affected by Japan's previous day's closing price.
Single latent variable capital asset pricing model.	Similar variables explain excess returns in the US and Japan; in the 1980s, US variables helped to explain Japanese excess returns; there was common co-movement of US and Japanese excess returns which indicate integration of these two markets.
Correlation analyses and unit root tests.	Generally, low correlation among markets which were higher in the latter period; no linkage among levels but there is among changes in stock market prices.
International capital asset pricing in which foreign investors are restricted to invest in the domestic equity market.	Mild segmentation hypothesis is supported.
Vector autoregression analysis.	High level of interdependence among markets; New York is the most influential, followed by Tokyo, then London and Paris; other European markets not influential and influenced by New York and Tokyo; European markets are not interdependent with each other.
Vector autoregression with impulse response and forecast variance decomposition analyses.	Substantial amount of interaction among markets; US is most influential then Switzerland and the UK; significant interaction among Australia, Canada, Hong Kong and the UK suggesting a British commonwealth factor; response to US shock: Canada and the UK respond without lag; France, Germany and Switzerland respond within 1 day; Australia and Japan take 2 days and are also significantly affected by UK shock; overall, international markets are informationally efficient.

Table 2.1 (continued)

Author(s) and Objective(s)	Type of Data and Period
• **Finnerty and Schneeweis (1979)** Analyses the co-movement of international equity and bond returns during a period of floating exchange rates.	Weekly stock market index levels, corporate bond yields, and exchange rates for the US, UK, West Germany, France, Belgium, Netherlands, Italy, Switzerland and Japan from April 1973 to July 1977.
• **Fischer and Palasvirta (1990)** Investigates the transmission of changes among different stock markets.	23 national stock market indices (includes US and 2 emerging markets — Malaysia and Mexico).
• **Hillard (1979)** Examines the equity market linkages during the period of the oil crisis in 1973–74.	Daily equity market data of Amsterdam, Paris, London, Milan, Frankfurt, New York, Sydney, Tokyo, Toronto and Zurich during the period 7 July 1973 to 30 April 1974.
• **Jeon and Von Furstenberg (1990)** Investigates structure of relationships among major equity markets.	Daily FT-Actuaries World Indices for New York, Tokyo, London and Frankfurt for the period 6 Jan. 1986 to 25 Nov. 1988.
• **Jorion and Schwartz (1986)** Investigates integration between the Canadian and US stock markets.	Monthly return on Canadian stocks from Laval Securities tape for the period Jan. 1963 to Dec. 1982.
• **King and Wadhwani (1990)** Investigates the linkages of stock markets during the Oct. 1987 crash.	High-frequency data from the stock markets of London, New York and Tokyo from July 1987 to Feb. 1988; also, daily returns in London for various subperiods during 1968–71.
• **King, et al. (1994)** Analyses of the time variation in the covariances and the integration between stock markets.	Monthly Morgan Stanley Capital International stock market indices for Australia, Austria, Belgium, Canada, Denmark, France, Germany, Italy, Japan, Netherlands, Norway, Spain, Sweden, Switzerland, UK and the US.
• **Koch and Koch (1993)** Examines the changes in relationships among national market indices since 1972.	Daily Morgan Stanley Capital International stock market indices for Japan, Australia, Hong Kong, Singapore, Switzerland, West Germany, the UK, and the US for 1972, 1980, and 1987.

Methods	Results
Correlation analyses.	Low correlation between US and foreign stock and long-term bond returns.
Cross-spectral analysis.	There is increasing interdependence among stock markets; US leads other markets.
Cross-spectral analysis.	High correlations among markets in the same continent but low correlations among markets between continents.
Vector autoregression analysis.	After the crash of 1987: here has been an increase in co-movements among stock markets, the influence of New York has decreased and the Tokyo market has become more independent from the other markets.
Capital Asset Pricing Model; maximum-likelihood estimation technique.	US and Canadian markets not integrated; sources of segmentation are legal barriers.
Contagion model of stock markets.	There is evidence of contagion effect among markets — larger volatilities lead to larger contagion effect just after the crash.
Multivariate factor model — dynamic version of the Arbitrage Pricing Theory; vector autoregression; autoregressive conditional heteroskedasticity.	Stock markets are not integrated.
Uses a structural, block-recursive, dynamic simultaneous equations model to capture contemporaneous as well as lead-lag relationships.	Growing interdependence; Japan's influence on other markets increased over the years while that of the US declined; most interactions are completed within 48 hours, and hence, intermarket relationships are informationally efficient.

Table 2.1 (continued)

Author(s) and Objective(s)	Type of Data and Period
• **Kwan, et al. (1996)** Examines the long-run and short-run linkages between equity markets.	Monthly stock market series for Australia, Hong Kong, Japan, Singapore, South Korea, Taiwan, the UK, the US and West Germany.
• **Marr, et al. (1991)** Investigates equity market integration based on US Euroequity offerings.	US Euroequity offerings from Jan. 1985 to Dec. 1988.
• **Ng, et al. (1991)** Examines volatility spill-over among five stock markets	Daily stock market data of the US (S&P500), Tokyo (Tokyo Stock Price Index), Korea (Composite Stock Price Index), Taiwan (Stock Exchange Weighted Stock Price Index) and Thailand (SET Index) from Jan. 1985 to Dec. 1987.
• **Smith, et al. (1995)** Investigates equity integration among eight stock markets using changes in risk/return ratios.	Monthly Morgan Stanley International Capital Perspective stock market indices for the US, Canada, UK, Japan, Germany, France, Switzerland, and Australia; 3-month: Treasury bill rate for the US, Canadian finance paper rate, Gensaki rate for Japan, French interbank loan rate, interbank loan rate for Switzerland and interbank sterling rate for Australia for the period Aug. 1980 to Sept. 1991.
• **Solnik (1991)** Examines the benefits of diversification within the Pacific-Basin markets.	Monthly stock market indices of Morgan Stanley Capital International for Australia, Japan, Hong Kong, Singapore/Malaysia, Korea, Taiwan, Thailand, Japan, US, UK, France, Germany, Europe, Far East and World for the period Dec. 1977 to Dec. 1988.
• **Stehle (1977)** Tests whether US stock market is segmented or integrated with other markets.	Monthly equity market data from the CRSP tape and stock price indices for Belgium, Canada, France, Germany, Italy, Japan, Netherlands, Switzerland, UK and the US.

Methods	Results
Granger-causality and cointegration.	No cointegration found among the markets. Bidirectional causality exists between Japan–South Korea, Singapore–Australia, Singapore–Hong Kong, Singapore–UK, Taiwan–Japan, Taiwan–Singapore, and Taiwan–South Korea. No market leads the US but the US leads Australia, Japan, Hong Kong and the UK.
Event study; probit regression.	Equity markets are integrated.
Autoregressive conditional heteroskedasticity (ARCH) model.	No volatility spill-over from the US to Taiwan and Korea; US volatility spill-over to Japan and Thailand occurred only after cross country investments were allowed in the latter two countries; hence, cross country investment is an important channel for the transmission of volatility among different national markets.
Utilises a model based on the Capital Asset Pricing Model that generates return-risk ratios for the different equity markets.	No full integration or equality of risk/return ratios between any of the equity markets.
Mean-variance and correlation analyses of local and US dollar returns.	Correlation of US returns with European returns is higher than with Pacific Basin returns; correlation of US with rest of the world is relatively low (0.43); exchange rate movements are not highly correlated with stock market returns; Korea, Taiwan and Thailand have low correlations with other markets; higher volatility of markets in later period (1985–88).
A version of the Capital Asset Pricing Model.	US equity market is neither segmented nor integrated with other stock markets.

Table 2.1 (continued)

Author(s) and Objective(s)	Type of Data and Period
• **To, et al. (1994)** Investigates the structure of interdependence between the emerging and major equity markets.	Monthly stock market data for Argentina, Brazil, Chile, Colombia, Greece, India, Jordan, Korea, Malaysia, Mexico, Nigeria, Pakistan, Philippines, Taiwan, Venezuela, Zimbabwe, Japan, UK and the US for 1976 to 1992.
	Monthly stock market data from Jan. 1960 to Dec. 1985 for the US (from CRSP) and for Australia, Austria, Belgium, Canada, Denmark, France, Germany, Hong Kong, Italy, Japan, Netherlands, Norway, Singapore, Spain, Sweden, Switzerland and UK (all from the Morgan Stanley Capital International Indices).

Methods	Results
Unit root, cointegration and vector autoregression analyses.	Increased interaction among markets occurred during 1985–92; US, UK and Japan influence Colombia, Greece, Mexico, Philippines, Taiwan and Thailand; US influences Brazil, Greece, India, Mexico, Malaysia, Philippines and Thailand; Japan affects Asian emerging markets, while the UK.'s effect is on African emerging markets; US is most influential market.
Consumption-based capital asset pricing model.	Hypothesis that markets are integrated could not be rejected but tests do not provide sufficient power to reject when deviations from the hypothesis are small.

3 Statistical Framework

Introduction

As previously stated, in examining the issue of equity market interdependence, the book uses cointegration, ECM, Granger-causality, variance decomposition, impulse response and ARCH model-based analyses which are all conducted within a VAR context. These techniques represent recent advances in time series econometrics. Cointegration analysis (Engle and Granger, 1987) is used to examine long-term relationships among the stock markets while the other techniques are utilised in the analyses of the short-term linkages between the markets. VAR is a non-structural model introduced by Sims (1980) which relies more on allowing the data to speak rather than on rigorous economic theory. The non-structural econometric modelling approach is particularly suited to the analysis of stock market relationships given the theoretical difficulties involved in capturing all the variables that affect equity market price.

"Cointegration among a set of variables implies that even if they are nonstationary, they never drift apart. In contrast, lack of cointegration suggests that such variables have no long-run link" (Arshanapalli and Doukas, 1993, p. 195). Cointegration analysis captures relationships among the levels of prices which are lost when other techniques are used because of the differencing which has to be done in order to achieve stationarity of variables. It also serves as a diagnostic test in order to prevent the occurrence of spurious regression. Cointegration is performed using the Johansen (1988) multivariate maximum likelihood procedure. This procedure has been shown to have certain distinct advantages over other procedures, e.g., Engle and Granger (1987) and Engle and Yoo (1987). If cointegration is found, error-correction models are constructed. These error-correction models (Engle and Granger, 1987) provide a basis for analysing the dynamics of the movement from short-term to long-term equilibrium among the equity markets' prices.

Granger-causality analysis pinpoints the direction of causation while the forecast variance decomposition and impulse response analyses, which are readily available within VAR, measure the duration and speed of interaction between the equity markets. A VAR is easy to estimate but it requires that the optimal lag length of each data series be determined and that each data series be stationary. To determine the optimal lag length, the likelihood ratio (LR) test is conducted. Each data series is tested for unit roots using the Augmented Dickey-Fuller (ADF) test in order to determine their stationarity.

An ARCH model-based (Engle, 1982) analysis is conducted in order to take into account the time varying conditional volatility which is a well-recognised property of stock market series. The initial intention was to perform the analysis using an ARCH model-based in the form of a VAR exponential generalised ARCH or VAR-EGARCH used in Koutmos (1996) and with origins from Nelson (1990). Due to a convergence problem, the analysis is limited to univariate ARCH/EGARCH models.

The econometric analyses are conducted in the following sequence (see Figure 3.1). A cointegration test is conducted first since the results from cointegration serve as inputs to the conduct of the Granger-causality test. The cointegration test, therefore, also serves as a diagnostic test for the Granger-causality test. If cointegration is found,

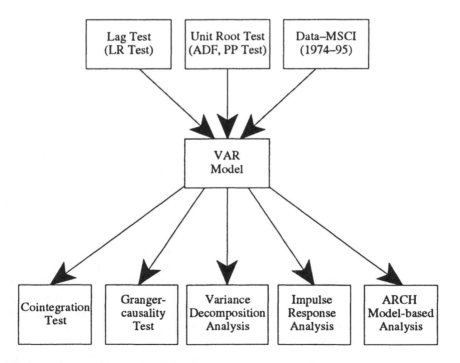

Figure 3.1 Econometric techniques and data used in the study

the Granger-causality, variance decomposition and impulse response analyses must be done based on error-correction models. If no cointegration is found, then the analyses will be based on the regression of the first differences of the variables using a standard VAR model. However, before cointegration can be done, the variables have to be tested for stationarity and optimum lags have to be determined. Finally, the ARCH model-based analysis is conducted. All the econometric analyses are conducted using weekly data covering the period 1975–95 based on the highly regarded Morgan Stanley Capital International (MSCI) indices.

This chapter discusses in detail the econometric techniques shown in Figure 3.1, except for the ARCH methodology which is explained in Chapter 7 of the book. The remaining part of this chapter is organised as follows. Firstly it discusses VAR in terms of its concept, model, requirements, strengths and weaknesses, and its use in equity market integration studies. It then explains the unit root test and lag test used in this study. This is followed by a discussion of cointegration and error-correction model construction, an explanation of Granger-causality and a discussion of forecast variance decomposition and impulse response analyses. Finally there is an explanation of the nature of the data used in this study before the conclusion to the chapter.

Vector Autoregression (VAR)

Non-structural Modelling

VAR is a form of non-structural econometric modelling introduced by Sims (1980) in response to difficulties associated with structural modelling. This subsection explains why non-structural modelling is appropriate in this study.

Equity price is affected by so many variables that it is difficult to capture all of these in a particular structural model (Officer and Finn, 1991). As mentioned earlier, previous research has generally used asset pricing models in constructing structural models to analyse equity market integration. However, as also shown earlier, these models have been subject to a number of theoretical, measurement, estimation and interpretation problems. Because of these reasons, it is therefore more appropriate to use a non-structural modelling approach. This approach does not rely on the use of a rigorous economic theory but more on what the data reveal. It has been shown in the existing literature (Granger, 1969; Sims, 1980; Engle and Granger, 1987) that non-structural models perform as well as structural econometric models.

Non-structural models avoid the problems of identification and exogeneity (see, Epstein, 1987 and Christ, 1993). The vector autoregression (VAR) which serves as the basis for all the econometric techniques used in this study exemplifies the non-structural modelling approach. VAR is discussed in more detail in the next section.

"It is normally claimed that structural models have greater predictive power as they include prior information. However, this is a matter of empirical judgement because while structural models include prior information, they also incorporate less sample information." (Dhrymes, 1973) Epstein (1987, p. 205) and Giles (1991, p. 5) have shown that "structural models have not performed better than non-structural models in the testing and modelling of price and financial behaviour".

Structural models continue to be beset with problems of identification and exogeneity. The usual suggested solution is to incorporate more economic theory. Sims (1980), however, challenged this reasoning. It has been "statistically verified that the economic theories represented by overidentifying restrictions are rejected in the vast majority of published tests" (Epstein, 1987, p. 206). Sims (1980), therefore, rejected all identifying restrictions and created a model in which no exogenous variables exist. Sims (1980) called this "alternative style of econometrics" a vector autoregression (VAR).

VAR therefore presents an entirely different approach to the analyses of economic relationships. It relies more on empiricism ("making the data speak") rather than on the guidance of "rigorous economic theory". In this regard, it is suited to the analysis of stock market relationships because of the present controversies that beset the use of asset pricing models in equity market integration. VAR is a way for stylising empirical regularities among time-series data. As Christ (1993, p. 76) puts it:

> In VAR, a set of observable variables is chosen, a maximum lag length is also chosen, and the current value of each variable is regressed on the lagged values of that variable and all other variables. No exogenous variables exist; all observable variables exist; all observable variables are treated as endogenous.

VAR Model

The following discussion comes from Judge, et al., 1988, pp. 753-754. A VAR process of order p[VAR(p)] for a system of M variables can be represented as follows:

$$y_t = c + \Theta_1 y_{t-1} + ... + \Theta_p y_{t-p} + v_t \qquad (3.1)$$

In this system of M equations, $c = (c_1,...,c_M)'$ is an M-dimensional vector, the

$$\Theta = \begin{bmatrix} \theta_{11,i} \cdots \theta_{1M,i} \\ \vdots \quad \cdot \quad \vdots \\ \theta_{M1,i} \cdots \theta_{MM,i} \end{bmatrix}$$

are $(M{\times}M)$ coefficient matrices and $v_t = (v_{1t},...,v_{Mt})'$ has the same stochastic properties as the reduced-form errors in a system of simultaneous equations. In other words, the v_t have mean zero, $E[v_t] = 0$ and the same (non-singular) covariance matrix $\sum_v = E[v_t v_t']$ for all t. Furthermore, v_t and v_s are uncorrelated for t≠s. A process v_t with these properties is often called *vector white noise* in analogy with the terminology used for the error process e_t.

Usually the parameters $c, \Theta_1, \Theta_2,...,\Theta_p$ and $\sum_v$ will be *unknown* in practice and have to be estimated from the available data before the process in Equation (3.1) can be used for forecasting and analysis purposes.

VAR requires that all variables are stationary. Hence, it is necessary to test each data series for stationarity. It is also necessary to determine the optimum lags for each variable.

Stationarity of VAR Process

The following discussion is taken from Judge, et al., 1988, p. 754. Stationarity is a property that ensures constancy of the means, variances, and autocovariances through time. A collection of M-dimensional random vectors $...,y_{t-1}, y_t, y_{t+1},...$ is called a *vector stochastic process*. Thus, for the moment the discussion is not restricted to VAR processes that are examples of vector stochastic processes.

A vector stochastic process is called *stationary* if:

(a) All the random vectors have the same mean vector $u, E[y_t] = u$ for all t.
(b) The variances of all involved random variables are finite, $var(y_{mt}) < \infty$ for $m = 1,...,M$ and all t.

(c) The covariance matrices of vectors y_t and y_{t+k} that are k periods apart do not depend on t but only on k.

$$\text{cov}(y_t, y_{t+k}) = E\left[(y_t - u)(y_{t+k} - u)'\right] = \Gamma_k \text{ for all } t$$

The last property implies for $k = 0$ that all vectors y_t have the same covariance matrix, that is, $E\left[(y_t - u)(y_t - u)'\right] = \sum_y$ for all t. For practical purposes, these conditions imply that the time series under consideration must not have trends, fixed seasonal patterns, or time-varying variances. Often data transformations will be necessary to ensure these properties.

It can be shown that a VAR(p) process is stationary if it has bounded means and covariance matrices and the polynomial defined by the determinant:

$$\det\left(I - \Theta_1 z - \Theta_2 z^2 - ... - \Theta_p z^p\right) \tag{3.2}$$

has all its roots outside the complex unit circle.

Estimation of VAR Processes

The following discussion is taken from Judge, et al, 1988, pp. 754-758. It was mentioned earlier that a VAR(p) model may be regarded as a reduced form of a simultaneous equation system. Equation (3.1) may therefore be written as follows:

$$\begin{aligned} y_{mt} = c_m &+ \Theta_{m1,1} y_{1,t-1} + ... + \Theta_{mM,1} y_{M,t-1} + ... \\ &+ \Theta_{m1,p} y_{1,t-p} + ... + \Theta_{mM,p} y_{M,t-p} + v_{mt} \end{aligned} \tag{3.3}$$

Assuming that T observations and p presample values for each of the variables, the vectors can be set up as:

$$y^m = \begin{bmatrix} y_{m1} \\ y_{m2} \\ \cdot \\ \cdot \\ y_{mT} \end{bmatrix}, y^m_{-i} = \begin{bmatrix} y_{m,1-i} \\ y_{m,2-i} \\ \cdot \\ \cdot \\ y_{m,T-i} \end{bmatrix}$$

for $i = 1,...,p$ and $m = 1,...,M$. In other words, $y^m - i$ contains the variables of the y^m vector lagged i periods. We also define $v^m = (v_{m1},...,v_{mT})'$. Using this notation, Equation (3.3) can be written as:

$$y^m = c_m j + \theta_{m1,1} y^1_{-1} + ... + \theta_{mM,1} y^M_{-1} + ... + \theta_{m1,p} y^1_{-p} + ... + \theta_{mM,p} y^M_{-p} + v^m$$

where j is a $(T \times 1)$ vector of ones. Compactly, this system can be written as:

$$y^m = X\theta_m + v^m \tag{3.4}$$

where:

$$X = \left[j, y^1_{-1}, ..., y^M_{-1}, y^M_{-2}, ..., y^M_{-2}, ..., y^1_{-p}, ..., y^M_{-p} \right]$$

and

$$\theta_m = \left[c_m, \theta_{m1,1}, ..., \theta_{mM,1}, \theta_{m1,2}, ..., \theta_{mM,2}, ..., \theta_{m1,p}, ..., \theta_{mM,p} \right]'$$

is the vector of coefficients in the mth equation of the system. Note that each of the M equations has the same regression matrix X. Writing the M equations as one system, we get:

$$y = (I_M \otimes X)\theta + v \tag{3.5}$$

where $\otimes$ denotes the Kronecker product. Under the assumptions previously stated, the covariance matrix of v is $E[vv'] = \sum_v \otimes I_T$

In such a system, the GLS estimator is identical to the LS estimator. This is in turn equivalent to estimating each equation separately by LS. Thus, without loss of estimation efficiency, each equation may be estimated by LS:

$$\hat{\theta}_m = (X'X)^{-1} X' y^m \tag{3.6}$$

For the complete system, the estimator:

$$\hat{\theta} = \left[I_M \otimes (X'X)^{-1} X' \right] y \tag{3.7}$$

is obtained.

To investigate the properties of this estimator, we assume that the v_t have a multivariate normal distribution $N\left(0, \sum_v \right)$ and v_t is independent of v_s for $s \neq t$. If, in addition, y_t is a stationary process, it can be shown that:

$$\operatorname{p\,lim}_{T \to \infty} \tfrac{1}{T} (X'X) = Q \tag{3.8}$$

is a nonsingular matrix and

$$\operatorname{p\,lim} \tfrac{1}{T} X' v^m = 0 \qquad m = 1, \ldots, M$$

Hence,

$$
\begin{aligned}
\operatorname{p\,lim} \hat{\theta}_m &= \operatorname{p\,lim}(X'X)^{-1} X' y^m \\
&= \operatorname{p\,lim}\left[(X'X)^{-1} X' \left(X\theta_m + v^m \right) \right] \\
&= \theta_m + \operatorname{p\,lim}\left(\frac{X'X}{T} \right)^{-1} \operatorname{p\,lim}\left(\frac{X'v^m}{T} \right) \\
&= \theta_m
\end{aligned}
$$

Consequently, each $\hat{\theta}_m$ is consistent and it follows that:

$$\operatorname{p\,lim} \hat{\theta} = \theta \tag{3.9}$$

Moreover, since the error process v_t is assumed to be normally distributed, $\hat{\theta}$ is asymptotically equivalent to the ML estimator and is therefore asymptotically efficient and normally distributed,

$$\sqrt{T}\left(\hat{\theta} - \theta \right)^d \to N\left(0, \sum_v \right) \tag{3.10}$$

The covariance matrix of the asymptotic distribution can be shown to be:

$$\sum_{\hat\theta} = \sum_v \otimes Q^{-1} \tag{3.11}$$

To estimate this matrix consistently, we need a consistent estimator of $\sum_v$. We use $(X'X/T)^{-1}$ as a consistent estimator of Q^{-1}. We can estimate the ijth element σ_{ij} of $\sum_v$ by:

$$\hat\sigma_{ij} = \frac{\left(y^i - X\hat\theta_i\right)\left(y^j - X\hat\theta_j\right)}{T - Mp - 1} \tag{3.12}$$

where in the denominator the number of parameters $Mp+1$ in each equation is subtracted from the sample size T. Denoting by $\overset{k}{\sum}_v$, the matrix with ijth element $\hat\sigma_{ij}$, a consistent estimator of $\overset{k}{\sum}_{\hat\theta}$ is:

$$\overset{k}{\sum}_{\hat\theta} = \overset{k}{\sum}_v \otimes (X'X/T)^{-1} \tag{3.13}$$

Note that this is an estimator of the asymptotic covariance matrix of $\sqrt{T}\left(\hat\theta - \theta\right)$. An approximation to the covariance matrix of $\hat\theta$ is:

$$\overset{k}{\sum}_v \otimes (X'X)^{-1} \tag{3.14}$$

In summary, "since there are no unlagged endogenous variables on the right-hand side, and since the right-hand-side variables are the same in each equation, the VAR model can be estimated using OLS. OLS is a consistent and efficient estimator. There would be no gain, for example, from using seemingly unrelated regression estimation" (Pindyck and Rubinfeld, 1991, p. 355).

Strengths and Weaknesses of VAR

VAR does not rely on robust economic theory and on assumptions about exogenous variables, in contrast to standard econometric models. Because of these properties, VAR is highly useful for forecasting purposes and there is evidence that it can outperform univariate models (Giles, 1991). It also makes VAR attractive to use considering that structural models have been shown to suffer from problems of misspecification (Eun and Shim, 1989; Epstein, 1987; Charemza and Deadman, 1992). The other major advantage of VAR is that it allows the determination of the structure of dynamic response to shocks within the system. This is done under the so-called variance decomposition and impulse response analyses. Lastly, VAR allows the testing of the independence of each block of lags corresponding to an individual variable about the relationship between a group of variables.

There are, however, certain important considerations that must be taken into account when using VAR. One of these is that VAR is dependent on a large number of observations. If there is only a small amount of data, then this may force the exclusion of certain variables and this is therefore tantamount to putting some restrictions on the system. VAR is also sensitive to lag length. This requires choosing the maximum lag length in such a way that problems with autocorrelation of the error term is avoided. Because VAR contains regressors which are lagged dependent variables, it is prone to autocorrelation of the disturbance term and hence, extra care must be taken in choosing the lag length (Charemza and Deadman, 1992, p. 1986). Lags have to be sufficiently long in order to avoid autocorrelation. However, long lags may hide the problem of omitted variables. Another factor that VAR is sensitive to is the ordering of variables. There are no formulas that provide guidance on how to determine the ordering of variables. This is left to the researcher's judgement and therefore the element of arbitrariness comes in (Judge, et al., 1988, p. 7676 and Lutkehpohl, 1993, p. 54). Finally, there is also the criticism that VAR modelling does not allow the researcher to understand the underlying economic process. It is claimed that this disregard for economic structure by VAR may hinder the development of new theories.

Unit Root Test and Lag Test

As stated earlier, VAR requires that all variables be stationary and that an optimum number of lags be determined. Hence, it is necessary to first test for the stationarity of each variable by conducting unit root tests. The optimum number of lags has to be tested also. The unit root and lag tests used in this study are discussed below.

Unit Root Test

Unit root tests determine whether each data series is nonstationary (i.e., unit roots exist) or stationary (unit roots do not exist). To do this, both the Augmented Dickey-Fuller or ADF for short (Said and Dickey, 1984) and the Phillips-Perron or PP for short (1988) tests are conducted. The null hypothesis of nonstationarity: H_0:$b_1 = 0$ (unit root) is tested in the following form of the ADF regression equations:

$$\Delta Y_t = b_0 + b_1 Y_{t-1} + \sum_{j=1}^{p} \theta_j \Delta Y_{t-j} + \varepsilon_t \qquad (3.15)$$

The test statistic to be calculated is the t-ratio but this statistic does not follow the usual Student t-distribution and has to be compared against critical values given in Fuller (1976). Both the original price level data and the first-differenced price level data are tested for unit roots.

The Phillips-Perron (1988) test "corrects for the serial correlation and autoregressive heteroskedasticity of the error terms" (To, et al, 1994). This test is used because it is considered to have a "wider applicability" (Kim, 1990). It is similar to the ADF test, except that instead of including lag terms to allow for serial correlation, it uses a nonparametric correction factor. The Shazam software which is used to perform the PP test utilises the Newey and West (1987) method in estimating this factor (White, 1993, p. 160). The critical values are the same as those of the ADF test.

Test of Lag Length

The optimum number of lags to be used in the VAR models is determined by the likelihood ratio test statistic which is calculated as follows:

$$LR = (T - c)(\log \det \Pi_r - \log \det \Pi_u) \qquad (3.16)$$

where Π_r and Π_u are the restricted $[(k-1)\text{lags}]$ and unrestricted (k lags) covariance matrices, T is the number of observations, and c is a correction factor used to improve small sample properties (Sims, 1980, p. 17) which is equal to the number of variables in each unrestricted equation in the system. LR is asymptotically distributed as a χ^2 with degrees of freedom equal to the number of restrictions.

Test statistic given by Equation (3.16) is used to test the null hypothesis of the number of lags being equal to $k-1$ against the alternative hypothesis that the number of lags is $k = 2, 3,...$ The test continues until the null hypothesis is accepted. The optimum lag corresponds to the lag when the null hypothesis is accepted.

Cointegration and Error Correction Model

Cointegration analysis in time series econometrics, introduced in the mid 1980s, has been regarded by many econometricians as the most important recent development in empirical modelling (Charemza and Deadman, 1992, p. 116). Cointegration analyses can indicate reliably whether there is a long-term equilibrium relationship between equity market indices. On the other hand, the error correction models (ECM) which are derived from cointegration, show how this equilibrium relationship is achieved. Cointegration shows the long-term relationship while the ECM indicates the short-term dynamics in the movement towards long-term equilibrium.[1] Cointegration analysis is conducted using the Johansen (1988) procedure.

This section briefly reviews the theoretical aspects and the strength and limitations of cointegration and error correction model analyses. The section is organised into four subsections. The first and second subsections discuss cointegration and error correction models, respectively. The third subsection presents an overview and a brief comparison of the different tests of cointegration while the last subsection summarises the strengths and limitations of cointegration and error correction model analyses.

Cointegration

When variables are cointegrated, even if each of them is nonstationary, they do not drift apart and hence, there is a long-term equilibrium relationship between the variables. The variables may deviate from this equilibrium over the short-term but this is just temporary as the necessary correction will be made.

When the series are cointegrated, there is no need to difference the variables, and thus there is no danger with having a spurious regression. Simple OLS and its standard associated tests become useful because as shown by Stock (1984), the least squares estimators converge to the true parameter faster than in the normal case. Therefore, cointegration analysis captures relationships among the levels of variables which are lost when other techniques are used because of the differencing which has to be done in order to achieve stationarity of the variables.

Cointegration is defined technically, following Engle and Granger (1987). Two non-stationary variables are cointegrated if a linear combination of the variables whose error term is stationary can be found. This can be formalised and extended into the multivariate case in the following manner. Suppose $Y_t = (Y_{1t}, Y_{2t}, ..., Y_{nt})$ denotes an n-dimensional vector. The components of Y_t are said to be cointegrated of order d,b denoted by $Y_t \sim CI(d,b)$ where $d > b > 0$ if (a) each component of Y_t is integrated of order d, and (b) there exists at least one vector $a = (a_1, a_2, ..., a_n)$ such that the linear combination $Y_t' a = a_1 Y_{1t} + a_2 Y_{2t} + ... + a_n Y_{nt} = u_t$ is integrated of order $(d - b)$. The vector a is called the "cointegrating vector". The number, r, of cointegrating vectors can be more than one and can go up to $n - 1$. A number of procedures have been proposed for determining r and these are discussed later in this chapter.

Error Correction Model

As stated earlier, cointegration implies that the variables are in long-run equilibrium. There could, however, be deviations from the equilibrium in the short run which will be transitory in nature. The ECM shows how short run deviations from equilibrium are corrected. "An ECM constitutes one case of a systematic disequilibrium adjustment process through which the two variables, Y and X, are prevented from 'drifting too far apart'. In such a process, Y changes in response to changes in X, and in addition, some proportion of any disequilibrium between target Y and actual Y is made up in any time period" (Perman, 1991, p. 4). The ECM, therefore, shows the short run dynamics of the adjustment towards long-term equilibrium. It also introduces a new channel of causality between X and Y.

Engle and Granger (1987) have shown by the error representation theorem that cointegrated variables imply an ECM with consistent coefficient estimates and standard errors of the estimates, and that regressing the first difference of cointegrated variables would result in misspecification error. What should be done in this case is to construct an ECM by including the lagged errors of the cointegrating regression as one of the independent variables in the new regression equation. Within a bivariate VAR context, this could take the following form:

$$\Delta Y_t = \sum_{j=1}^{n} b_j \Delta X_{t-j} + \sum_{j=1}^{n} c_j \Delta Y_{t-j} + \phi e_{t-1} + w_t \qquad (3.17)$$

where e_{t-1} are the lagged residuals from the level form of Equation (3.17).

In Equation (3.17), if some of the b_js are statistically significant, then current changes in Y can be explained by past changes in the other series, thus indicating the presence of a causality relationship. Furthermore, even if the b_js are not statistically significant but the ϕs are, then X and Y have a common trend "which implies that the current change in Y may be due to the movement of X towards alignment with the trend value of Y. Thus, a new channel of causality can emerge. Such causality cannot be detected without the use of cointegration or error correction models" (Lin and Swanson, 1993, pp. 615 and 617).

"The ECM was conceived by Sargan in 1964 and brought into popularity by Engle and Granger (1987). There are three major views on the ECM — that of Phillips, Sargan-Hendry, and Engle-Granger. The first two approaches seem to share a common philosophy that ECMs are structural representations of the dynamic adjustments towards equilibrium defined by economic theory. On the other hand, Engle-Granger view ECM as statistical representation of a movement towards an equilibrium defined in a statistical sense. For the first two approaches, the parameters in the ECM have theoretical bases; for Engle-Granger, this is not necessary. All of these approaches, however, assign a limited role to economic theory. They all have the objective of estimating a conditional distribution rather than a given theoretical model. The first two approaches estimate a conditional distribution based on current and lagged values while the last approach assumes that the conditional distribution is just based on lagged values" (Alogoskoufis and Smith, 1995, p. 151). This book adopts the Engle-Granger view.

Testing for Cointegration: Johansen Procedure versus Others

A number of methods for testing cointegration have been proposed. Among the more commonly used are the (a) DF or ADF test on u_t estimated from the cointegrating regression, called the Engle and Granger (1987) two-step procedure, (b) Engle and Yoo (1987) extension on the Engle and Granger approach, called the Engle and Yoo three-step procedure and (c) Johansen (1988) maximum likelihood approach. Cointegration analysis was developed within the context of the Engle-Granger (1987) approach which remains popular until now. The Engle-Yoo (1987) three-step procedure had started to eat into the popularity of the two-step approach since 1989, and lately, the Johansen (1988) approach is becoming the standard approach to cointegration. It is quite well-accepted now that the multivariate VAR, maximum likelihood Johansen approach overcomes major problems associated with the two-step and three-step procedures (Davidson and MacKinnon, 1993, p. 726).

Engle-Granger (1987) and Engle-Yoo (1987) procedures The Engle-Granger procedure is easy to conduct. However, it has several major defects. First, the result of this procedure can be affected by, the ordering of variables. When variables are cointegrated, the ordering should not matter. If X is found to be cointegrated with Y, then Y should also be cointegrated with X. The Engle-Granger procedure does not fulfil this. The result depends on which variable is used in normalisation. This becomes more problematic when the model is multivariate. Another problem that comes up is that the Engle-Granger procedure cannot distinguish between one or more cointegrating vectors as it assumes that the cointegrating vector is unique. Finally, because the procedure requires two steps, an error made in the first step gets to be carried to the second step. The Engle-Yoo (1987) procedure makes improvements on the Engle-Granger (1987) approach by proposing an additional step. By doing so, they showed that this approach achieves the same limiting distribution as the full-information likelihood method (Aggarwal, et al., 1995, p. 109).

These two procedures have also been criticised by Phillips and Ouliaris (1990) and Johansen (1988) as being relatively weak tests. When variables are affected by several common stochastic systems, univariate tests misspecify the model and will therefore result in cointegration test results that are biased as shown by Ma (1993) in his criticism of Taylor and Tonks (1989).

Johansen (1988) procedure The Johansen (1988) full-information (FI) maximum likelihood (ML) procedure, provides a more generalised approach to cointegration that overcomes the problems associated with the first two approaches. It is not burdened with the normalisation problem and is thus able to handle the situation in which there are more than one cointegrating vector. It "gives consistent ML estimates of the whole cointegrating matrix, and produces a likelihood-ratio statistics for the maximum number of distinct equilibrium vectors in the matrix which makes it possible to identify the whole set of cointegrating relationships using this method. Another advantage offered by the ML estimator is that the LR test statistic has an exact known distribution which is a function of just one parameter. Given these distribution properties of the ML estimator, specification tests can be carried out on the cointegrating vectors" (Perman, 1991, p. 17).

The Johansen (1988) procedure can be shown as follows. Assuming the following VAR model:

$$Y_t = A_1 Y_{t-1} + A_2 Y_{t-2} + ... + A_k Y_{t-k} + \varepsilon_t$$

In difference form, this becomes:

$$\Delta Y_t = \sum_{i=1}^{k-1} \pi_i \Delta Y_{t-i} + \pi Y_{t-k} + \varepsilon_t$$

where:

$$\pi = -\left(I - \sum_{i=1}^{k} A_i \right)$$

$$\pi_i = -\left(I - \sum_{j=1}^{i} A_j \right)$$

the likelihood-ratio test for the presence of at most $n-1$ cointegrating vectors is:

$$\lambda_{trace}(r) = -T \sum_{i=r+1}^{n} \ln\left(1 - \hat{\lambda}_i\right) \tag{3.18}$$

where:

$\hat{\lambda}_i$ = the estimated values of the characteristics roots obtained from the π matrix

T = the number of useable observations

The key feature of Equation (3.18) is that the rank of the matrix π is equal to the number of independent cointegrating vectors. For example, if rank $(\pi) = 1$, then there is a single cointegrating vector and πY_{t-k} is the error correction factor. For $1 < \text{rank}(\pi) < n$, the conclusion would be that there are multiple cointegrating vectors. The test statistic, Equation (3.18), tests the null hypothesis on the number of distinct cointegrating vectors such as $r = 0$ versus $r > 0$, $r \leq 1$ versus $r > 1$ and so on. The critical trace values are given in Johansen and Juselius (1990), Appendix, Table A3, p. 209. Extended values can be found in Osterwald-Lenum (1992), Table 1, p. 467.

As mentioned earlier, in order to implement the Johansen procedure, the LR and ADF tests are first conducted to determine the optimal lag length and stationarity of each of the data series. Each of these tests have previously been discussed.

Further Comments on Cointegration Analysis

In analysing economic and financial time series, cointegration plays a very important role.

(a) Cointegration also serves as a form of misspecification test. If the given time series are not cointegrated, a broader set of variables could be tested to see if this is still the case. On the other hand, if the given set of time series turn out to be cointegrated, it has been shown by Engle and Granger (1987) that a VAR in the first differences of the variables would be misspecified and an ECM would have to be constructed.

(b) "Economic theory suggests possible equilibrium relationships between variables, but tends to inform us very little concerning the adjustment process at work. If a postulated equilibrium relationship exists, then the variables specified in that relationship should be cointegrated. Testing for cointegration is, therefore, a test for the existence of the equilibrium relationship postulated, and hence of whether the model is well-defined. These remarks apply both where the model being considered is a single equation, and also where we are interested in the long-run properties of a system of equation." (Perman, 1991, pp. 20–21) In this particular study, if the Australian equity market is found to be cointegrated with the other markets, then this would imply the predictability of Australian stock prices, thus, indicating that this group of equity markets are not "efficient". Furthermore, within an ECM representation, if the Australian equity market turns out to have a significant ECM variable, then this would imply that the Australian equity market is significantly related to the other markets in the long-run and that it adjusts with the other market in the short run whenever there is departure from this long-run relationship.

(c) "A cointegrating vector gives us directly highly consistent estimates of long-run equilibrium vectors. These estimates have good properties without the need to make any prior assumptions about the dynamics in the data-generating mechanisms. Cointegration analysis may also be viewed as a simplifying device in model design. The estimation of long-run equilibrium properties of models may, thus, be analysed abstracting from the model's short-term dynamic structure. The theory underlying cointegration analysis justifies the omission of short-run dynamics in the estimation of long-run parameters" (see Clements, 1989, p. 29).

Granger-causality

A variable X "Granger-causes" Y if (a) past values of X explain Y, (b) but past values of Y do not explain X (Granger, 1969). This is the case if the null hypothesis is rejected in the following set of equations.

(a) If the variables are not cointegrated:

H_0:X does not cause Y (all $b_j = 0$)

H_A:X causes Y (at least one $b_j \neq 0$ and all $b_j^* = 0$)

$$\Delta Y_t = \sum_{j=1}^{n} b_j \Delta X_{t-j} + \sum_{j=1}^{n} c_j \Delta Y_{t-j} + u_{t-1} \qquad (3.19)$$

$$\Delta X_t = \sum_{j=1}^{n} b_j^* \Delta Y_{t-j} + \sum_{j=1}^{n} c_j^* \Delta X_{t-j} + u_{t-1}^* \qquad (3.20)$$

(b) On the other hand, if the variables are cointegrated:

H_0:X does not cause Y (all $b_j = 0$ and $\phi = 0$)

H_A:X causes Y (at least one $b_j \neq 0$ and/or $\phi \neq 0$)

$$\Delta Y_t = \sum_{j=1}^{n} b_j \Delta X_{t-j} + \sum_{j=1}^{n} c_j \Delta Y_{t-j} + \phi e_{t-1} + w_t \qquad (3.21)$$

$$\Delta X_t = \sum_{j=1}^{n} b_j^* \Delta Y_{t-j} + \sum_{j=1}^{n} c_j^* \Delta X_{t-j} + \phi^* e_{t-1} + w_t^* \qquad (3.22)$$

where e_{t-1} are the lagged residuals from the level form of Equation (3.19).

The Granger-causality test is based on the F-statistic which is calculated for each equation using the restricted and unrestricted form of each equation:

$$F = \frac{\left(SSE_R - SSE_{UR}\right)/n}{SSE_{UR}/\left(N-2n\right)} \qquad (3.23)$$

where:

SSE_R, SSE_{UR} = residual sum of squares of the restricted and unrestricted models
N = total number of observations
n = number of lags

If some of the b_js are statistically significant, the current changes in a stock market index series can be explained by past changes in the other stock market series, thus indicating the presence of a causality relationship. As previously stated, "even if the b_js are not statistically significant but the ϕs are, then X and Y have a common trend "which implies that the current change in Y may be due to the movement of X towards alignment with the trend value of Y. Such causality cannot be detected without the use of cointegration or error correction models" (Lin and Swanson, 1993, pp. 615 and 617).

Forecast Variance Decomposition and Impulse Response Analyses

This discussion follows that of Eun and Shim (1989). Suppose the following VAR model is given:

$$Y(t) = C + \sum_{s=1}^{m} A(s)Y(t-s) + e(t) \qquad (3.24)$$

In order to analyse how a random shock in a particular market affects prices in other markets, the VAR model has to be expressed as a moving average representation, since the $e(t)$s, although serially uncorrelated, are also contemporaneously correlated. This is done through successive substituting of $e(t)$s in place of $Y(t-s)$. Assuming the process is stationary, the following equation is obtained:

$$Y(t) = \sum_{s=0}^{\infty} B(s)e(t-s) \qquad (3.25)$$

The system of equations in (3.25) now expresses the price in each market as a function of its past innovations and the price innovations from other markets.

The structure of response of each market to a unit shock in another market within s periods can be determined by transforming the innovations into orthogonalised innovations through Cholesky decomposition (see Appendix of Eun and Shim, 1989, for details) which is done as follows: Let $e = Vu$ where $V = $ a lower triangular matrix and $u = $ orthogonalised innovations such that $E(ee') = S$, $VV' = S$ and $u(t)$ has an identity covariance matrix. Equation (3.25) then becomes:

$$Y(t) = \sum_{s=0}^{\infty} B(s)Vu(t-s)$$

$$= \sum_{s=0}^{\infty} C(s)\,u(t-s) \tag{3.26}$$

Each element in $C(s)$ represents the response of a particular market to a shock of one standard error in another market within s period(s). This is called the "impulse" response of that market.

The forecast variance of each market's price can also be broken up into portions accounted for by shocks or price innovations coming from other markets. This is provided by $\sum_{s=0}^{T} C_{ij}(s)$ which is obtained from Equation (3.26). This element represents the proportion of forecast error variance of Y_i which is due to innovations in Y_j.

Data and Calculations

As previously stated, data on the markets being investigated are obtained from Morgan Stanley Capital International (MSCI). The MSCI indices for different markets are computed using the same formula which is value weighted and are therefore comparable. MSCI calculates national stock market indices for 22 developed and 23 emerging markets using the same criteria and formula. The stocks in the MSCI index are value weighted, i.e., the weight of each stock in the index is based on its proportion to the total market value of all the stocks included in the index. The MSCI index captures 60 per cent of the total stock market capitalisation of each country. Weekly data are obtained for all the markets being studied. The data covered the period 27 December 1974 to 8 December 1995 for the US, UK, Japan, Australia, Hong Kong and Singapore and 1 January 1988 to 8 December 1995 for Korea, Taiwan, Malaysia, Indonesia, Philippines and Thailand.

All calculations are performed using the following econometric softwares: SHAZAM (White, 1993) for the unit root tests, and RATS (Doan, 1992 and 1995) for the lag test, cointegration, Granger-causality, forecast variance decomposition, impulse response function, and ARCH model analyses.

Conclusion

This chapter discusses in detail the different time series techniques that are used in the book. These techniques are cointegration, error correction model, Granger-causality, forecast variance decomposition and impulse response analyses. Since all these techniques are conducted within a vector autoregression (VAR) framework which represents a non-structural approach to econometric modelling, a discussion on VAR and non-structural modelling is also presented. Finally, since the book uses the MSCI data, the advantages of the MSCI indices which arise from the way they are constructed, are explained in this chapter.

Note

1   "The use of the term 'equilibrium' is unfortunate since economic theorists and econometricians use the term in different ways. Economic theorists usually employ the term to refer to an equality between desired and actual transactions. The econometric use of the term makes reference to any long-run (i.e., equilibrium) relationship among nonstationary variables. Cointegration does not require that the long-run (i.e., equilibrium) relationship be generated by market forces or the behavioural rules of individuals. In Engle and Granger's use of the term, the equilibrium relationship may be casual, behavioural, or simply a reduced-form relationship among similarly trending variables (Enders, 1995, pp. 358–360). Within the cointegration literature, all that is meant by equilibrium is that it is an observed relationship which has, on average, been maintained by a set of variables for a long period." (Cuthbertson, et al., 1992, p. 132)

4 Price Interdependence between the Equity Markets of Australia and its Major Trading Partners

Introduction

This chapter investigates the specific issue of equity markets price linkage between Australia and its major trading partners — the US, UK, Japan, Hong Kong, Singapore, Taiwan and Korea, both in the long-run and in the short-run using cointegration based on the Johansen (1988) procedure, Granger-causality, forecast variance decomposition and impulse response analyses which were discussed in detail in Chapter 3. This issue has great practical and policy significance. Before the onset of the current financial crisis in Asia, Australian investors were looking to Asia as a venue for portfolio diversification (see, The Australian, 22 February 1994). Based on portfolio diversification theory, it is important that investors are aware of the extent of financial integration between Australia and Asia. If the Australian and Asian equity markets are less than fully integrated, then the latter can serve as good avenues for Australian investment diversification. From a policy perspective, this knowledge is also important. If Australian and Asian equity market prices are found to be closely-linked, there is a danger that shocks in one market may spill over to other markets (the so-called "contagion effect" — see King and Wadhwani, 1990). Hence, this may require closer cooperation between the prudential and monetary regulators of all these markets if these effects are to be avoided or minimised.

Traditionally, Australia's major economic partners, in terms of trade and investment, have been the United States and the United Kingdom. However, over the last decade and a half, the bulk of Australia's trade has shifted from the US and the UK to Asia — particularly to Japan, Korea, Hong Kong, Singapore, and Taiwan (see Garnaut, 1989 and DFAT, 1992a, 1992b). Although the US and the UK still remain significant partners, Japan now accounts for the largest share of Australia's trade. Trade with Korea, Taiwan, Hong Kong and Singapore continues to grow at a substantial rate. Australia has therefore become more economically integrated with these Asian countries in terms of trade. Because of this, there is an expectation that the financial markets of Australia and these Asian countries have also become integrated. This expectation is bolstered by the advent of deregulation in each of these countries which has led to the removal or substantial lowering of regulatory restrictions and barriers to the movement of capital between countries and within countries. Working against this, however, is the fact that the levels of cross country investment between Australia and these countries, although increasing, remains at a relatively much lower level than the level of trade interaction (Garnaut, 1989 and DFAT, 1992a, 1992b). Hence, the question remains as to whether, indeed, the financial markets of Australia and these Asian countries are integrated.

The US and the UK equity markets, on the other hand, not only remain as significant trading partners, but are in fact also the major investment partners of Australia (Garnaut, 1989 and DFAT, 1992a, 1992b). These two markets are also the largest and third largest in the world, and as such, they are, in the words of Espitia and Santamaria (1994), "net information generators". They are therefore expected to influence significantly Australia and the other markets. Previous studies (for instance, Eun and Shim, 1989; Espitia and Santamaria, 1994; and McNelis, 1993) have found the US market to be the most influential equity market in the world. Eun and Shim (1989) had found the UK market to be influential on the Australian market which was attributed to the so-called "commonwealth factor". With the shift in Australia's trading pattern, the financial deregulation of Australian and Asian markets, and the stock market crash of 1987, it would be interesting to find out whether these two markets continue to be influential on the Australian market.

Very few studies have been done on Australia's equity market linkage with other countries and the bulk of these have concentrated on Australia's linkage with the developed markets of the US, UK, Japan, Canada and Germany. This study differs from and has the following advantages over previous studies:

(a) It takes an Australian perspective and focuses on Australia's interaction with Japan, Hong Kong, Singapore, Korea, Taiwan, US, and the UK. Previous studies (e.g., McNelis, 1993), as mentioned earlier, focused on Australia's linkage with the developed markets. A recent study by Kwan, et al. (1995) dwells on these markets but this is not done from an Australian perspective. Furthermore, as will be discussed later, the present study uses a methodology that offers more advantages than the methodology used by the said study.

(b) The present study performs cointegration tests using the Johansen (1988) procedure. Previous studies (e.g. Kwan, et al., 1995; McNelis, 1993) used procedures which are considered to be less reliable than the Johansen procedure.[1]

(c) The present study uses the MSCI index which, as previously explained in Chapter 3, provides for comparability and avoids the problem with double-listed stocks. Previous studies (e.g. Kwan, et al., 1995) have used other indices which are subject to the problems of double-listing and/or non-comparability.

(d) It uses weekly data rather than daily data. Daily data are subject to the problems of having too much noise (Bailey and Stulz, 1990), nonsynchronous trading and day of the week effects.

The results from this chapter therefore provide new, robust and more comprehensive evidence in relation to the issue of Australia's equity market integration with its major trading partners.

The issue of equity market price interdependence between Australia and its major trading partners is investigated during three subperiods: before financial deregulation (1974–83), before the stock market crash (1984–87) and after the crash (1988–95). No cointegration was found in each of the three subperiods. The Granger-causality and forecast variance decomposition analyses reveal that Australia is significantly linked with the US, the UK, and Hong Kong in the short-run. The US and the UK are influential on Australia while Australia is influential on Hong Kong. The impulse response analyses further reveal that Australia responds to shocks from the US and the UK immediately during the first week. Hong Kong also responds to an Australian shock during week 1. The interaction between Australia and these markets is completed within a period of four weeks. Thus, the equity markets of Australia and its trading partners are not significantly linked in the long-run. However, in the short-run, Australia's equity market has significant linkages with the US, UK and Hong Kong markets.

This chapter is organised as follows. First, a discussion of the institutional setting is provided in terms of trade and investment interaction, financial deregulation and comparative features of the different stock markets being investigated. This is followed by a presentation, discussion and analysis of the empirical results. A conclusion is then provided at the end of the chapter.

Institutional Setting

This section reviews the trends and patterns of trade and investment interaction between Australia and its major trading partners. It also broadly reviews the deregulation which occurred in each of these markets. Finally, this section makes a brief comparison of the major features of the different equity markets.

In terms of trade and investment interaction, the US, UK, Japan, Hong Kong, Singapore, Taiwan and Korea account for the bulk of Australia's foreign trade. Among this group, the US, UK, and Japan are the three largest trading partners of Australia. Australia's trade had shifted away from the US and the UK to Asia. The US and UK share of Australia's trade had declined while that of Asia had significantly increased, particularly that of Korea. While trade between Australia and Asia is substantial, investment interaction remains at a very low level. Australia's investment partners continue to be the US and the UK. Although Japan is a significant investment partner of Australia, it is far behind the US and the UK.

Substantial financial deregulation had occurred in all markets. The US, Singapore and Hong Kong deregulated ahead of the others going as far back as the second half of the 1970s. Japan, Australia and the UK had theirs in the first half of the 1980s while Taiwan and Korea only started theirs, in a much more limited extent, towards the end of the 1980s. Deregulation had led to the removal of significant controls on interest rates, capital flows across borders, financial activities, in the amount of and the way credit was allocated, commissions, and foreign entry into the stock market. As a result of deregulation, with the exception of Taiwan and Korea, all the stock markets have become relatively open and liberalised. There are, however, certain significant restrictions that still remain. An example of this is the separation of banking and securities business in the US and Japan. Also, in spite of deregulation, markets are far from being internationalised. Only London and Singapore can be considered as truly international markets. The rest, including the US market, are far from being so.

The eight equity markets included in this study account for about 95 per cent of world market capitalisation. In fact, the US, Japan and the UK equity markets are the three largest stock markets in the world. The other stock markets, i.e. Australia, Hong Kong, Singapore, Korea and Taiwan which are more or less comparable in terms of size are far smaller in size compared to the US, Japan and UK stock markets. In terms of turnover, the US, Japan and UK are also the top three markets in the world, while Taiwan and Korea are relatively significant markets, being ranked 4th and 6th, in the world in 1993, respectively.

In terms of trading, clearance and settlements systems, these markets have mostly become computerised. The US, Japanese and Australian markets are dominated by institutional investors while the Hong Kong, Singaporean, Korean and Taiwanese markets mainly consist of individual investors. Price-earning (P/E) ratios vary across markets with Japan having the highest and Hong Kong the lowest. Commissions are negotiable in the US, UK, Hong Kong and Singapore but are fixed in Japan, Korea, and Taiwan. With the exception of the US which is specialist-driven, all the other markets are market-driven. There are also price limits in Japan, Taiwan and Korea but none in the other markets.

Trade and Investment Interaction

Trade interaction Australia is heavily involved in terms of trade with the US, UK, Japan, Hong Kong, Singapore, Taiwan and Korea. As shown in Figure 4.1, the total share of these countries, as a group, in Australia's trade averaged around 56 per cent annually during the period

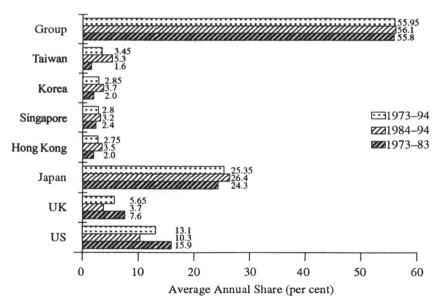

Source: DFAT, *The APEC Region Trade and Investment*, 1995; *Composition of Trade*, 1993; *Direction of Trade*, 1971–72 to 1988–89

Figure 4.1 Average annual share in Australia's total trade: 1973–94

1973–94. Among this group, Japan had the biggest share (25 per cent) followed by the US (13 per cent) and then by the UK (5 per cent). The others had a far smaller share. It can also be seen in Figure 4.1 that Australia's trade had shifted to Asia away from the US and the UK. Comparing the period 1973–83 and 1984–94, the US and the UK shares of Australia's trade had substantially decreased while that of each of the Asian countries had significantly increased. The US share had declined from 16 per cent to 10 per cent and that of the UK had decreased by almost half from 7 per cent to 4 per cent. On the other hand, Korea's share had increased from 1 per cent to 5 per cent; Taiwan — from 2 per cent to 4 per cent; Hong Kong — from 2 per cent to 4 per cent; and Japan — from 24 per cent to 26 per cent.

As can be seen in Figure 4.2, Australia had a negative balance of trade with these countries, as a group, during the period 1973–94. This was primarily due to Australia's trade with the US and the UK which had been in deficit during the whole period. Australia's trade balance with the Asian countries had generally been in surplus. The only Asian countries in which Australia had incurred negative balance of trade are

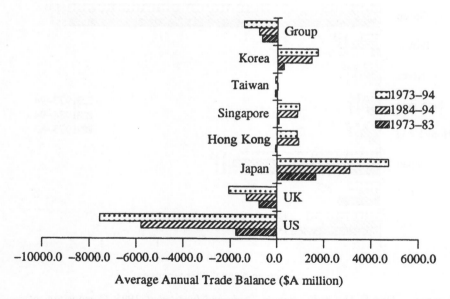

Source: DFAT, *The APEC Region Trade and Investment*, 1995; *Composition of Trade*, 1993; *Direction of Trade*, 1971–72 to 1988–89

Figure 4.2 Australia's average annual trade balance with selected countries

Taiwan (for the whole period) and Hong Kong (only during the period 1973–84). Thus, it can be said that Australia generally had favourable trade balances with Asia and negative balances with the US and the UK.

Investment interaction   Australia's investment interaction with Asia occurred at a very much lower level as compared with its trade interaction. Australia's main investment relationships were with the UK and the US and with Japan to a certain extent. Australia's investment interaction with the other countries had been much less significant. Australia was a net recipient of investment from all countries, except Korea. The net level of investment from the US, Japan and Hong Kong had increased while the one from Singapore and Korea had decreased.

Portfolio investment dominates (64.6 per cent of total investment in mid 1990) Asia's investment in Australia. These portfolio investments are mostly in the form of bonds rather than equities (DFAT, 1992a, pp. 63–64). The same pattern goes with Australia's investment in Asia where portfolio investment accounts for an even higher percentage (82 per cent) of the total.

Although Australia's direct investment in Japan is relatively lower, Japan is the biggest destination for Australia's portfolio investment in Asia. In mid 1990, Japan was the third largest foreign investor in Australia accounting for almost 18 per cent of total non-official foreign investment (DFAT, 1992a, pp. 63–64). Japanese portfolio investment was 2.5 times greater than direct investment but a small proportion of this has been in equities (ibid.). Among Hong Kong, Korea and Taiwan, only Hong Kong has substantial investment in Australia. Furthermore, in Asia, only Hong Kong is a significant destination for Australian direct foreign investment.

Financial Deregulation

Financial deregulation refers to the lessening or removal of regulations in financial markets, usually, for the purpose of allowing a greater operation of market forces and competition in guiding the activities within these markets. Substantial financial deregulation has occurred in all markets over the period 1975–95 although Taiwan and Korea only started theirs in the late 1980s and are still saddled by significant regulations. Financial deregulation started in the US, Hong Kong and Singapore as early as the second half of the 1970s. The UK followed in 1979 and Japan started theirs in 1980. Australia had its deregulation in 1983. Deregulation had basically led to the removal of significant controls on interest rates, capital flows across borders, financial activities, in the amount of and the way credit was allocated, commissions, and foreign entry into the stock market. As a result of financial deregulation, the US, UK, Japan and Australia have become relatively open and liberalised markets in terms of inflows and outflows of capital.

Prior to deregulation, markets were burdened mainly by interest rate control, financial market segmentation, and credit ceilings and allocation. These controls were instituted for any or a combination of the following reasons: protection of savers and/or investors, protecting the stability and profitability of financial institutions, controlling money supply or conducting monetary policy, assisting the development of certain selected sectors or industries in the economy, and political/military reasons. These controls, however, led to undesirable consequences on the economy of each country in terms of discouragement of savings, inability by small borrowers to obtain funds, rent seeking, and economic concentration, bias towards expansionary monetary policy, nationalisation or government dominance of the banking business, concentration of assets in certain areas and a mismatch of assets and liabilities of financial institutions, limited funding sources for business, especially for long-term needs, and the growth of the informal financial sector. These unwanted effects of deregulation, coupled with the move towards the floating exchange rate and the oil crisis in 1973 which resulted in volatility of exchange rates, and volatility in inflation and interest rates brought about measures from governments which were aimed at removing these controls and freeing the movement of capital.

The progress of deregulation in these countries has been hastened by two factors: regulatory arbitrage and foreign government pressure. Investors and users of capital are attracted to markets with the least regulations and hence, in order to compete for financial business, markets saddled with regulations are forced to deregulate (Honeygold, 1989, pp. 12–13; Shapiro, 1992, p. 569). Foreign government (i.e., the US) pressure has been a significant factor in the opening up of the Japanese, Taiwanese and Korean markets to international influences.

During the decade 1983–94, in terms of regulatory aspects affecting access to their capital markets, the group of countries that is the focus of this study may be grouped into three categories, following Rhee (1992):

(a) those whose capital markets have always been generally liberal and open to entry by foreign firms;

(b) those whose capital markets were previously restricted to the foreign sector but which are now fully liberalised except for restrictions on certain sectors;

(c) those whose capital markets are in the process of opening up to foreign institutions.

Hong Kong and Singapore may be classified under the first category. As shown earlier, these two countries have always pursued a philosophy of liberalisation and internationalisation in their capital markets, and through this strategy, have established themselves as international financial centres. They have generally followed a policy of attracting foreign financial institutions through minimum restrictions on the activities of these institutions. They have had no foreign exchange control and have always offered very attractive withholding tax incentives to foreign financial institutions.

On the other hand, Australia, Japan, Taiwan and Korea all have a history of protectionism of their economy and their capital markets. However, as discussed previously, these countries have implemented financial reforms and deregulation and as a result of these, Australia and Japan can be classified now under category (b). Taiwan and Korea, however, fall under category (c).

In terms of the equity markets, a very important deregulatory measure has been the abolition of fixed commissions which occurred in the US in 1975, in Australia in 1984 and in the UK in 1986. This measure led to the reduction in commissions in these markets and has considerably lowered transaction costs. Another important deregulatory measure has been the abolition of segmentation of certain activities. In 1986, the segmentation between brokers and jobbers in the UK was removed, and in Australia, brokers were allowed to advertise their services starting in 1984. Finally, equity markets were opened to foreign participation. Foreign securities companies were allowed to obtain licenses and to purchase local securities companies in the UK, Japan and Australia in 1984. In Korea, since 1983, foreign securities firms have been allowed to establish local offices as well as to acquire up to 10 per cent of the ownership of domestic securities firms. Korean companies have also been allowed to open representative offices abroad. The same measure was implemented in Taiwan in 1988.

Comparative Features of Equity Markets

This section compares the different markets in terms of size, trading, clearance and settlement system, institutionalisation, price-earning ratios, and commission structure.

Capitalisation and turnover As a group, the eight markets included in this study, account for 95 per cent of world capitalisation. Figure 4.3 shows the share of each market in total world capitalisation (bars) and the world ranking of each based on capitalisation (number above each bar).

As can be seen in Figure 4.3, the US, Japan and the UK are the world's top three stock markets. These three alone, taken together, already account for about 88 per cent of the total world capitalisation. The other stock markets, i.e. Australia, Hong Kong, Singapore, Taiwan and Korea, are relatively far smaller in size. As shown in Figure 4.3, among this group, Hong Kong is the biggest, followed by Australia. Figure 4.4 further shows that, in terms of market capitalisation, Australia used to be bigger than Hong Kong until 1991. In 1992, Hong Kong overtook Australia.

Figure 4.5 indicates the turnover ratio (bar) and world ranking in terms of turnover volume (number above each bar) for each market. The figure shows that the US, Japan and the UK are also the top three

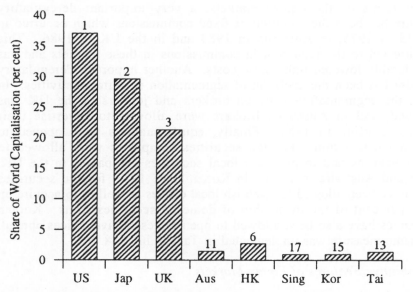

Source: *Emerging Stock Markets Factbook*, 1994, as cited in Bos and Fetherston, 1995, p. 3

Figure 4.3 Share of world capitalisation and rank, 1993

stock markets in terms of turnover volume. However, with the other markets, a different picture emerges. They are not of comparable size any more in terms of turnover. Taiwan and Korea have much bigger turnover than the others making them ranked, respectively, fourth and sixth worldwide which are much higher than the world ranking they have in terms of capitalisation. Australia and Hong Kong have relatively lower turnover.

Trading system Except for the US and Japan which are specialist-driven, all the other markets are market or order-driven. There are price limits in Japan, Taiwan and Korea but not in the other markets. Daily limits could range from 10 to 30 per cent of the previous day's closing price in Japan and even much higher in Taiwan and Korea (Naughton, 1999, p. 29). Trading in all markets have become mainly computerised. Japan, however, still use the open outcry method for the 150 most active stocks. Computerisation of trading started in Singapore in 1988, Hong Kong in 1992, Australia in 1990, Taiwan in 1985, Korea in 1988, US in 1971, UK in 1986 and Japan in 1981. These computerised trading systems have been given different names: SEATS

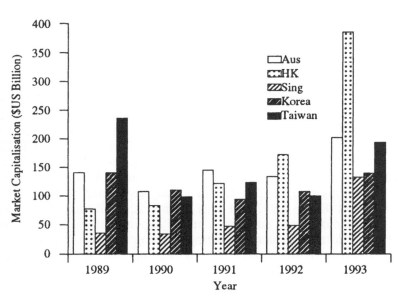

Source: Australian Stock Exchange, *Monthly Index Analysis*, 31 May 1994, no. 171, p. 46

Figure 4.4 Market capitalisation, 1989–93

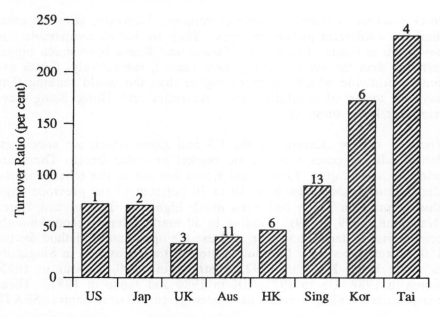

Source: *Emerging Stock Markets Factbook*, 1994, as cited in Bos and Fetherston, 1995, p. 3

Figure 4.5 Turnover ratio and world ranking on turnover volume, 1993

(Stock Exchange Automated Trading System) in Australia, CORES (Computer-assisted Order Routing and Execution System) and FORES (Floor Order Routing and Execution System) in Japan, AMS (Automatic Order Matching and Execution System) in Hong Kong, CLOB (Computerised Central Limit Order Book) in Singapore, SMATS (Stock Market Automated Trading System) in Korea, and CATS (Computer-Assisted Trading System) in Taiwan. In a study conducted by Domowitz (1990), cited in Rhee (1992), it was found that automated trading systems benefit customers but this is at the expense of market makers who lose about 6 to 9 per cent of average trading prices. Rhee (1992), however, expressed the concern that automation also increases systematic risks in the equity market

Clearance and settlements system Clearance and settlements have also been computerised which make possible settlement within a period of one to three days after sale or purchase of a stock. Settlement used to take at least a week in these markets before the advent of computerisation. Korea is leading the way in terms of efficiency of trade settlement. CHESS (Clearing House Sub-Register System) in Australia started in 1991; JASDEC (Japan Securities Depository Centre) in Japan implemented in 1991; CCASS (Central Clearing and Settlement System) in Hong Kong in 1992; CDP (Central Depository Pte) in Singapore in 1990; KSDC (Korea Securities Depository Corporation) in Korea in 1974; and TSDC (Taiwan Securities Central Depository Co.) in Taiwan in 1990. Leung (1991) classifies Hong Kong and Australia as being in the developmental stage and Japan, Korea, Singapore and Taiwan as being in the mature stage.

Institutionalisation   The main investors in the US, UK, Australian and Japanese equity markets are institutions, such as pension funds, insurance companies, investment companies, bank trusts, and foundations. Institutions had actually previously accounted for a smaller proportion of share ownership in these markets. In 1949, the proportion of share ownership by institutions was only 13 per cent in the US, 31 per cent in Japan, and 20 per cent in Australia. By the 1990s, this proportion had increased to almost 50 per cent in the US, 78 per cent in Japan, and a staggering 90 per cent in Australia (Fabozzi and Modigliani, 1992, p. 225; Tashiro and Osman, 1996, p. 251; Drake and Stammer, 1993, p. 297). On the other hand, the Hong Kong, Singaporean, Taiwanese and Korean stock markets are dominated by individuals who could actually be representing family companies. In 1991, the proportion of share ownership of individuals was about 51 per cent in Korea and 54 per cent in Taiwan. Figures are not available for Hong Kong and Singapore, but anecdotal evidence gathered by researchers, e.g. Harwood and Takahashi (1996) point to the dominance of individual shareholders.

Price-earnings (P/E) ratios   As shown in Figure 4.6, there is a huge discrepancy in P/E ratios among the markets. P/E ratios are highest in Japan and lowest in the UK. The high P/E ratios in Japan is accounted for by a different accounting system and the presence of interlocking companies which result in "double counting and crossholdings". It has been found that after adjusting for accounting differences and crossholdings, the effective Japanese P/E ratios are comparable to those of the US (The Economist, 22–28 February 1992, p. 74).

Commission structure   Negotiable commissions are in place in the US, UK and Australia. The US moved to this in 1975, the UK in 1986 and Australia in 1984. In Japan, it is both fixed and negotiable. In Hong Kong, it is fixed while in Singapore it is staggered. Commissions have been made variable in the US, UK, Australia, Hong Kong and Singapore but still remain fixed in Japan, Korea and Taiwan.

A summary of the comparative features of the equity markets of Australia and the other countries is given in Table 4.1.

Internationalisation   The substantial decrease in regulatory and information barriers brought about by the rapid progress of deregulation would have encouraged more internationalisation of national markets. Hong Kong and Singapore are very much already integrated into the global financial system.   Korea and Taiwan, however, are still not actively linked to the global financial markets due to the residue of certain regulations (OECD, 1990).   In terms of equity markets, the London Stock Exchange is the most international (Table 4.2).   New York is still very much domestic in orientation (see O'Brien, 1992, p. 44 and Tucker, et al., 1991, p. 158).   Tokyo is fast internationalising since its deregulation in 1980.   The Foreign Stock Section of the Tokyo Stock Exchange has grown fast since the second half of 1980.   In Taiwan and Korea, foreign entry into these markets is still at an early

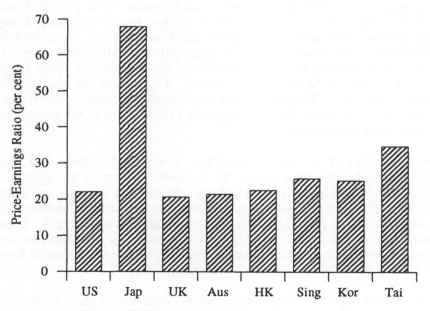

Source: *Emerging Stock Markets Factbook*, 1994

Figure 4.6 Price-earnings ratio, 1993

Table 4.1   Major institutional features of US, UK, Australian and selected Asian equity markets

Features	US	Japan	UK	Australia	Hong Kong	Singapore	Korea	Taiwan
Market capitalisation as per cent of world capitalisation*	37.05	29.62	21.27	1.45	2.73	0.94	0.99	1.38
Market capitalisation (world ranking*)	1	2	3	11	6	17	15	13
Turnover (ratio*)	72.2	71.0	33.4	40	47.2	89.8	172.2	235.5
Turnover volume (world ranking*)	1	2	3	14	11	13	6	4
Official specialists	Yes	Yes	No	No	No	No	No	No
Automated quotations	Yes	Yes	Yes	Yes	Yes	Yes	Yes	Yes
Computer-directed trading	Yes	Yes	Yes	Yes	Yes	Yes	Yes	Yes
Price limits	None	Yes	None	None	None	None	Yes	Yes
Transaction tax per cent (round-trip*)	0	0.5	0.55	0.6	0.6+	0.5	0.6+	0.14
Price-earning ratio*	22.1	67.8	20.7	21.5	22.6	25.8	25.12	34.7
Main investors (institution or individual)	Inst.	Inst.	Inst.	Inst.	Indiv.	Indiv.	Indiv.	Indiv.

*   1993 data

Source: Richard Roll (1989), "The International Crash of October 1987", *Black Monday and the Future of Financial Markets*, Homewood, IL: Dow Jones Irwin, 1989, as cited in Eiteman, et al. (1992), p. 350 as cited in Eiteman, et al. (1992), p. 350; Rhee (1992); *Emerging Stock Markets Factbook* (1994) as cited in Bos and Fetherston, 1995, p. 3

stage. Although foreign financial institutions have been able to establish domestic branches, they have yet to become active participants in these countries' financial markets. Finally, in Australia, it has been said that in terms of regulatory restrictions, the country's financial markets are relatively fully accessible to foreign participation. However, in spite of this, the level of internationalisation of the country's equity as well as other financial markets remain relatively low in comparison to Hong Kong, Singapore or even Japan. Very few foreign securities firms have found success in their operations in the Australian market. Also, there are very few Australian securities houses operating overseas, although out of this few, there is a thrust towards Asia. In terms of foreign listing, the market share of foreign securities traded on the Australian Stock Exchange in 1989 was a meagre 2.4 per cent. This only goes to show that the Australian equity market, is one which is still predominantly domestic in orientation.

Hypothesis Testing Results

Data used Weekly data from 27 December 1974 to 8 December 1995 are used for Australia, Japan, Hong, Singapore, the US and the UK, while weekly data from 2 January 1988 to 8 December 1995 are utilised for Taiwan and Korea. The analyses of data take into account two major structural breaks: financial deregulation in Australia in 1983 and the

Table 4.2   Foreign shares listing in selected equity markets, 1989

Stock exchange	Total number of stocks listed	Number of foreign stocks listed	Percentage of foreign stocks listed
New York	1681	74	4.4
UK	2656	595	22.4
Australia	1506	47	3.1
Singapore	326	194	59.5

Source: *Institutional Investor*, March 1989, pp. 197–204 as cited in Tucker, et al., 1991, p. 158

stock market crash of 1987. In this regard the data is broken up into four subperiods: before financial deregulation (1974–83), and after deregulation, before the stock market crash (2 January 1984 to 16 October 1987) and after the crash (2 November 1988 to 8 December 1995). The week during the crash (17–23 October 1987) and the week after the crash (24–30 October 1987) are excluded as these two weeks represent abnormal movements in the equity markets. Since the data for Taiwan and Korea are available only starting on 1 January 1988, the after crash subperiod has been looked at in two separate groups of countries.

Thus, the following four separate data analyses are conducted:

(a) Before deregulation (27 December 1974 to 30 December 1983) for Australia, Japan, Hong Kong, Singapore, the US and the UK.
(b) After deregulation but before the crash of 1987 (2 January 1984 to 16 October 1987) for Australia, Hong Kong, Singapore, the US and the UK.
(c) After the crash of 1987 (2 November 1987 to 8 December 1995) for Australia, Hong Kong, Singapore, the US and the UK.
(d) After the crash of 1987 (1 January 1988 to 8 December 1995) for Australia, Hong Kong, Singapore, the US, the UK, Taiwan and Korea.

Expected results In terms of cointegration, it is expected that Australia will not be cointegrated with the other markets during the period before deregulation but will be cointegrated with the other markets during the period after deregulation both before the crash and after the crash. Previous research has shown that markets which were not linked to other markets before financial deregulation have become linked after deregulation. An example is the case of Thailand, as found by Ng, et al. (1991) and the UK, as discovered by Taylor and Tonks (1989). It has also been found that markets became more integrated after the crash. This has been the experience of Japan and the US (Campbell and Hamao, 1992; Malliaris and Urrutia, 1992).

In terms of Granger-causality and forecast variance decomposition analyses, it is expected that the Australian market will be influenced by the US and the UK, in line with existing evidence (Eun and Shim, 1989 and McNelis, 1993), but will not have any causal relation with Korea and Taiwan, as these markets are still heavily regulated. These markets have been found not to be linked to other markets by Ng, et al. (1991) and Cheung and Mak (1992), among others. The impulse response analysis is expected to show that most of the interaction between Australia and these markets should occur within a period of one week.

Previous studies (Malliaris and Urrutia, 1992; Eun and Shim, 1989; and Espitia and Santamaria, 1994) have found that the international transmission of information between markets is completed within a period of two days.

Unit Root Test Results

The null hypothesis of nonstationarity (unit root) and alternative hypothesis of stationarity (no unit root) are tested for each data series, in original form and in first-differenced form, using the ADF and PP tests previously discussed. Equation (3.15) was estimated and the corresponding t-statistic for b_1 was calculated for each of the data series. The different calculated t-statistics are presented in Tables 4.3 and 4.4. The critical t-value obtained from Fuller (1976) is -2.57. Table 4.3 presents the computed t-statistics for all the series in their original level.

As can be seen in this table, none of the computed t-statistics are significant and hence all the stock market original indices in all subperiods are nonstationary. On the other hand, Table 4.4 shows that the t-statistics corresponding to the first-differenced form of the series are all significant which means that in first-differenced form, all the series are stationary. All these results therefore show that each data series is integrated of order 1 or I(1).

Optimum Lag Test Results

Some studies (Eun and Shim, 1989; Espitia and Santamaria, 1994) have found that information from one national market spill-over to other national markets within a period of one week. Hence, using Equation (3.16), lags of 1 versus 2 are first tested ($H_0:k=1$ versus $H_A:k=2$). If the null hypothesis is rejected, the test continues by testing the next higher lags until the null hypothesis is accepted. The results are presented in Table 4.5. The results show that a lag of 3 was significant in the period before the crash (2/1/84–16/10/87) while a lag of 1 was significant in all the other periods.

Cointegration Test Results

Since the unit root test results showed that each of the data series is I(1), the cointegration test using the Johansen (1988) procedure is therefore conducted. Using Equation (3.18), the trace statistics are calculated to test the null hypothesis of $r=0$ versus the alternative hypothesis of $r>0$. The computed trace statistics are given in Table 4.6. None of the values are significant which means that the Australian equity market is not cointegrated with the other equity markets. Thus, there is no stationary long-run relationship between the equity market of Australia and that of the US, UK, Japan, Hong Kong, Singapore, Taiwan and Korea.

Table 4.3 **Results of ADF and PP tests based on price levels for different subperiods Australia and its major trading partners**
(H_0: unit root versus H_A: no unit root)

Series	27/12/74–30/12/83		2/1/84–16/10/87		2/11/87–8/12/95		1/1/88–8/12/95	
	ADF	PP	ADF	PP	ADF	PP	ADF	PP
Aus	−1.44	−1.21	1.52	1.89	−2.03	−2.02	−1.71	−1.70
Japan	0.28	−0.11	1.32	1.03	−1.89	−1.79	−1.85	−1.76
HK	−1.46	−1.72	2.20	2.17	−0.42	−0.65	−0.47	−0.63
Sing	−0.34	−0.58	−0.61	0.16	−0.36	−0.50	−0.36	−0.51
UK	−0.84	−1.94	0.77	1.10	−1.44	−1.44	−0.58	−1.20
US	−1.94	−1.04	−0.96	−0.44	0.89	1.13	0.89	1.03
Korea							−1.40	−1.61
Taiwan							−2.56	−2.18

* critical value (10 per cent level): −2.57

Table 4.4 **Results of ADF and PP tests based on price level difference for different subperiods Australia and its major trading partners**
(H_0: unit root versus H_A: no unit root)

Series	27/12/74–30/12/83		2/1/84–16/10/87		2/11/87–8/12/95		1/1/88–8/12/95	
	ADF	PP	ADF	PP	ADF	PP	ADF	PP
Aus	−3.60	−17.71	−4.22	−11.99	−4.72	−21.06	−4.76	−20.72
Japan	−5.78	−19.80	−3.65	−10.32	−5.37	−20.79	−5.58	−20.51
HK	−4.82	−18.14	−4.90	−12.99	−5.50	−19.91	−5.44	−19.73
Sing	−4.24	−18.73	−3.54	−12.74	−4.61	−18.05	−4.55	−17.96
UK	−5.03	−21.94	−3.27	−14.22	−6.60	−21.09	−6.61	−20.93
US	−4.38	−21.90	−3.68	−11.58	−4.81	−23.42	−4.64	−23.37
Korea							−5.23	−18.92
Taiwan							−4.88	−19.59

* critical value (10 per cent level): −2.57

Table 4.5 Results of likelihood ratio test Australia and its major trading partners

| Period | Lags | | | | | |
| | 1 versus 2 | | 2 versus 3 | | 3 versus 4 | |
	LR-value	P-value	LR-value	P-value	LR-value	P-value
Before deregulation (27/12/74–30/12/83)	38.29	0.3659				
Before crash (2/1/84–16/10/87)	53.32	0.0315*	59.32	0.0085*	43.29	0.1881
After crash–6 countries (2/11/87–8/12/95)	33.75	0.5761				
After crash–8 countries (1/1/88–8/12/95)	65.43	0.4268				

* significant at the 10 per cent level

Table 4.6 Computed trace values Australia and its major trading partners $H_0:r=0$ versus $H_A:r>0$

Period	Trace values	Critical values* (10 per cent level of significance)
27/12/74–30/12/83	4.6877	89.48
6/1/84–16/10/87	40.0864	89.48
6/11/87–8/12/95	2.8735	89.48
1/1/88–8/12/95	27.6215	118.50

* from Osterwald–Lenum (1992), Table 1, p. 467

Granger-causality Test Results

Since no cointegration exists between the different time series, the Granger-causality test was performed based on Equations (3.19) and (3.20). Based on Equation (3.23), F-statistics are calculated to test the null hypothesis that X does not affect Y (H_0: all $b_j = 0$) against the alternative hypothesis that X→Y (H_A: at least one $b_j \neq 0$). The null hypothesis that Y does not affect X (H_0: all $b_j = 0$) versus the alternative hypothesis that Y→X (H_A: at least one $b_j \neq 0$) is also tested. The calculated F-statistics are presented in Table 4.7. The only values that are significant are those that correspond to the US→Australia linkage for the periods (27/12/74–30/12/83), (2/11/87–8/12/95), and (1/1/88–8/12/95). Based on these results, it can therefore be said that in the short-run, Australia is only significantly linked to the US and that the US is influential on Australia. It should be noted though that the US market did not influence the Australian market during the period before the crash. This is possibly because the Australian market was still adjusting to the impact of the 1983 financial deregulation. By 1988, however, the Australian market had resumed its usual linkage with the US market.

Table 4.7   Calculated F-statistics based on equations (3.19) and (3.20) Australia and its major trading partners (for each market, top row: X→Y, bottom row: Y→X, (P-values are in parentheses)

Market (X)	Aus (Y) (27/12/74– 30/12/83)	(2/1/84– 16/10/87)	(2/11/87– 8/12/95)	(1/1/88– 8/12/95)
Japan	0.0474 (0.8277)	0.1783 (0.6733)	0.0177 (0.8943)	0.0038 (0.9510)
	0.0659 (0.7975)	0.3342 (0.5687)	2.3650 (0.1248)	0.0158 (0.8999)
HK	1.4621 (0.2272)	1.1182 (0.2917)	0.3098 (0.5781)	0.4683 (0.4942)
	0.0256 (0.3365)	0.5859 (0.4450)	0.0002 (0.9895)	0.4739 (0.4916)
Sing	0.4061 (0.5242)	0.3007 (0.5841)	0.6587 (0.4175)	0.9690 (0.3255)
	0.0001 (0.9906)	2.3468 (0.1272)	0.2698 (0.6038)	0.4638 (0.4962)
UK	0.2546 (0.6141)	0.4633 (0.4969)	2.1320 (0.1450)	1.9598 (0.1623)
	0.2560 (0.6131)	0.1956 (0.6588)	1.1205 (0.2904)	0.0535 (0.8172)
US	7.4502*(0.0066)	1.3310 (0.2501)	8.7435*(0.0032)	6.9673*(0.0086)
	0.4866 (0.4858)	0.0049 (0.9443)	0.6399 (0.4242)	0.0535 (0.8172)
Korea	–	–	–	1.5783 (0.2097)
				0.2566 (0.6127)
Taiwan	–	–	–	0.0790 (0.7788)
				1.1360 (0.2871)

* significant at the 1 per cent level

Forecast Variance Decomposition and Impulse Response Analyses Results

Forecast variance decomposition analyses results   The forecast variance decomposition analysis focuses on the effect of factors other than past prices, i.e. random shocks on the price in each market. This can therefore show how influential other markets are on Australia and vice versa. The results of the forecast variance decomposition analyses are presented in Table 4.8 for the three subperiods. The numbers on each row show the percentage breakdown of the forecast variance of the market in that row according to sources while the numbers on each column show the percentage contribution of that market to the forecast error variance of each market. The Australia row shows five lines of numbers corresponding to the period before deregulation (BD), before crash (BC), after crash for 6 markets (AC-6), and after crash for 8 markets (AC-8), and the average for all the four lines. The numbers corresponding to the intersection of the Australian row and the Australian column show the percentage of Australia's forecast variance that is due to random shocks coming from itself. For instance, looking at the BD (before deregulation) line the number corresponding to the Australian column is 73.51 per cent. This means that during the period before deregulation, 73.51 per cent of the Australian forecast variance was due to random shocks coming from itself. This percentage goes up to 89.67 per cent during the period before the crash (Australian row, BC line, Australian column). The percentages were 84.44 per cent (AC-6) and 85.04 per cent (AC-8) after the crash. Thus, it can be said that after deregulation, the proportion of Australia's forecast variance that were due to other markets decreased. This means that the Australian market became less affected by foreign markets after deregulation.

The numbers corresponding to the intersection between the Australian row and the column pertaining to a particular market show the percentage of the Australian forecast variance that is due to that market. Looking at the intersections between the Australian row and each of the columns, it can be seen that the US and the UK are the markets that most heavily influenced Australia. On average, for the three periods, the US accounted for 7.80 per cent of Australia's forecast error variance, while the UK contributed 6.59 per cent. All the other markets had relatively small impact on Australia. The influence of the Australian market over other markets is shown by the numbers on the Australian column in Table 4.8. It can be seen in this particular column that Australia's biggest impact was on Hong Kong (average of 4.09 per cent for three periods). Although Australia was only the third most

Table 4.8   Forecast variance decomposition analyses Australia and its major trading partners (4-week period forecasting horizon)

Market expl.	Period*	By innovation in							
		Aust	Japan	HK	Sing	UK	US	Tai	Kor
Auat	BD	73.51	3.51	0.17	0.07	8.91	13.84		
	BC	89.67	2.50	0.73	0.75	4.50	1.87		
	AC-6	84.44	0.57	0.19	0.12	6.54	8.14		
	AC-8	85.04	0.52	0.23	0.16	6.42	7.33	0.03	0.28
	Ave.	83.17	1.78	0.33	0.28	6.59	7.80	0.01	0.07
Japan	BD	0.02	88.53	0.00	0.11	4.65	6.70		
	BC	0.32	87.10	0.88	0.73	5.09	5.89		
	AC-6	0.56	84.22	0.19	0.02	10.58	4.43		
	AC-8	0.47	84.09	0.21	0.02	10.40	4.14	0.23	0.45
	Ave.	0.34	85.99	0.32	0.22	7.68	5.29	0.06	0.11
HK	BD	2.89	3.69	79.63	1.33	3.66	8.79		
	BC	4.97	0.87	88.63	2.12	1.66	1.74		
	AC-6	4.28	0.17	86.25	0.08	5.74	3.48		
	AC-8	4.21	0.17	86.15	0.10	5.67	3.00	0.02	0.68
	Ave.	4.09	1.23	85.17	0.91	4.18	4.25	0.02	0.68
Sing	BD	0.27	2.37	12.39	66.40	5.94	12.63		
	BC	2.66	2.24	10.40	80.02	0.56	4.12		
	AC-6	1.22	2.38	18.61	62.11	7.97	7.72		
	AC-8	1.27	2.37	18.14	62.49	8.00	6.87	0.01	0.85
	Ave.	1.36	2.34	14.89	67.76	5.62	7.84	0.01	0.85
UK	BD	0.02	0.09	0.19	0.46	86.02	13.23		
	BC	0.63	1.42	0.53	1.30	86.93	9.19		
	AC-6	0.27	0.54	0.10	0.08	86.45	12.55		
	AC-8	0.14	0.53	0.14	0.10	87.32	11.43	0.29	0.08
	Ave.	0.27	0.65	0.24	0.49	86.68	11.60	0.29	0.08
US	BD	0.04	0.00	0.24	0.01	0.00	99.71		
	BC	3.86	3.86	0.58	1.82	0.21	92.17		
	AC-6	0.15	0.02	0.04	0.13	0.29	99.37		
	AC-8	0.02	0.01	0.05	0.15	0.31	99.12	0.23	0.12
	Ave.	1.02	0.97	0.23	0.53	0.20	97.59	0.23	0.12
Tai	AC-8	0.66	0.94	1.49	1.17	0.41	0.07	94.58	0.69
Kor	AC-8	0.12	2.21	2.42	0.54	0.98	1.19	0.48	92.05

* BD = before deregulation (6 markets); BC=before crash (6 markets);
  AC = after crash for 6 markets; AC-8 = after crash for 8 markets
  Ave. = average

influential market on Hong Kong, its influence was very close to that of the two most influential markets — the US (4.25 per cent — intersection between the US column and HK row) and the UK (4.18 per cent — intersection between the UK column and HK row). Australia's influence on other markets were much smaller or can be considered negligible: 0.34 per cent on Japan, 1.36 per cent on Singapore, 0.27 per cent on the UK and 0.66 per cent on Taiwan. Hence, random shocks emanating from Australia were only influential on the Hong Kong market. Thus, in summary, the forecast variance decomposition analyses revealed that Australia is significantly influenced by the US and the UK and that Australia is influential on the Hong Kong market.

Impulse response analyses results It has been found earlier that the Australian market has significant relationships with the US, UK, and Hong Kong markets. This section further investigates this relationship by analysing the speed and length of time of the interaction between the Australian market and these other markets. This is done through the impulse response analyses. The results of the analyses are shown in Figures 4.7, 4.8 and 4.9. Figure 4.7 shows the response of the Australian market to shocks coming from the US market. It can be seen that Australia immediately responds to a US shock within the first

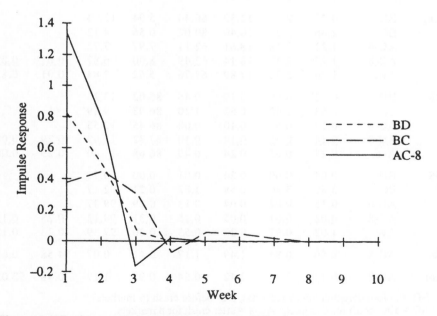

Figure 4.7 Australia's response to a US shock

week and generally completes its response within four weeks, except during the period before the crash where it took eight weeks to complete its response. Australia's response to the US shock had been generally positive, with some negative responses occurring on week 4 during the period before the crash and on week 3 during the period after the crash. No negative response occurred during the period before deregulation.

Figure 4.8 illustrates Australia's response to a UK shock. Australia also responds to a UK shock immediately on the first week. It finishes most of its responses within a period of four weeks. The only exception to this is during the period before the crash where Australia took seven to eight weeks to complete its response. During the period after the crash, all of Australia's responses were positive. However, in other periods, both positive and negative responses were registered. For the period before the crash, a negative response was made during week 3, and during the period before deregulation, on weeks 3 to 9.

Figure 4.9 shows Hong Kong's response to random shocks from Australia. Hong Kong immediately responds to an Australian shock during the first week and most of its responses are completed within a period of four weeks, with the exception of the period before the crash,

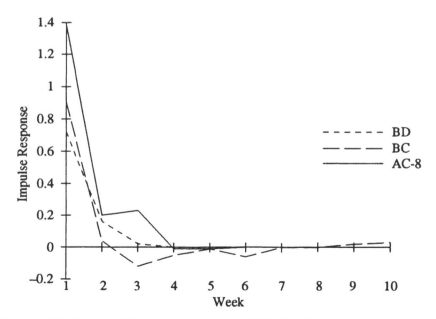

Figure 4.8 Australia's response to a UK shock

where Hong Kong's response continued until week 9. Generally, Hong Kong responded positively to an Australian shock, except for the period after the crash where negative responses occurred during week 3.

Recapitulating, the impulse response analyses showed that Australia responds to a US and UK shock immediately on week 1. The same response is shown by Hong Kong to an Australian shock. Generally, the interactions are positive and are completed within a period of four weeks.

Conclusion

The cointegration test results show that the Australian equity market is not significantly linked with any other equity market in the long-run. On the other hand, the Granger-causality and forecast variance decomposition analyses revealed that Australia has significant linkages with the US, the UK and Hong Kong over the short-run. This confirms the results of previous studies (Eun and Shim, 1989; Kwan, et al., 1996;

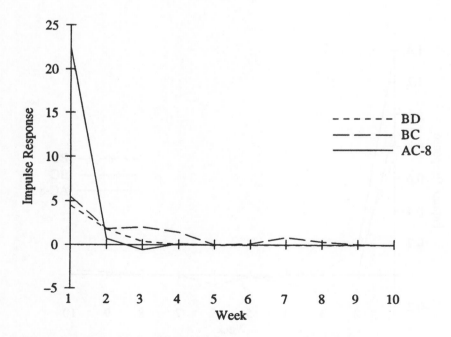

Figure 4.9 Hong Kong's response to an Australian shock

and McNelis, 1993). The impulse response analyses showed that the interaction between Australia and these markets occur mostly within a period of four weeks. The Australian equity market is therefore linked to the US and UK in the short-run but not in the long-run. This could imply that the Australian equity market overreacts to movements of past prices in the US and UK but this overreaction gets to be corrected over the long-run. The study shows that the US is influential on Australia but Japan is not. This could be interpreted as evidence supporting the claim that the US market is influential worldwide but Japan is not, even at the regional level (Eun and Shim, 1989; Espitia and Santamaria, 1994; Cheung and Mak, 1992). The lack of cointegration between the equity markets of Australia and the US, UK, Hong Kong, Singapore, Taiwan and Korea means that the latter markets could serve as good avenues for long-term portfolio diversification by Australian investors. In the short-term, Australian investors can reap portfolio diversification benefits from using the markets of Japan, Singapore, Taiwan and Korea.

Note

1   Kwan et al (1996) used pairwise Dickey-Fuller tests while McNelis (1990) used vector autoregression but did not adjust for cointegration. The Johansen procedure is well-accepted in the literature to be superior to the DF tests. As shown by Engle and Granger (1987), failure to adjust for cointegration will result in misspecification error.

5 Price Interdependence among the ASEAN Equity Markets

Introduction

This chapter investigates the extent and structure of price linkages among five Association of Southeast Asian Nations (ASEAN) markets (Malaysia, Singapore, Philippines, Indonesia and Thailand), both in the long-run and in the short-run using cointegration based on the Johansen (1988) procedure, Granger-causality, forecast variance decomposition and impulse response analyses. The ASEAN region member economies' growth rates are among the highest in the world (DFAT, 1992). Starting in 1988, as a result of financial reforms arising out of deregulation (Cargill, et al., 1986; Greenwood, 1986; Pringle, 1987; Drake, 1986; and Cole, 1988), the financial markets of these countries have also grown significantly (Fry, 1995; Allen, 1991). As a result, this group of markets has been attracting the attention of investors worldwide, as demonstrated by the increasing number of mutual funds specialising on ASEAN including the Asia Pacific Fund, the Malaysia Fund and the Thai Fund in the US and London capital markets (Rhee, 1992). A crucial piece of information that investors need for purposes of portfolio diversification is the degree of linkage among these markets. Unfortunately, this information is unknown at present. There has been an increasing intensity of trade between these countries (Ariff, 1996) suggesting that their financial markets are also becoming increasingly linked. The relatively few studies on financial integration on Asia have primarily focused on Japan and the so-called Asian tigers or dynamic economies of Hong Kong, Singapore, Taiwan and Korea (see, for instance, Hung and Cheung, 1995; Kwan, et al., 1996; Kwok, 1995; Cheung and Mak, 1992; among others). The current author is unaware of any systematic study which has been undertaken on equity market linkages among ASEAN countries. This study therefore seeks to redress this deficiency.

If the ASEAN markets are found to be cointegrated, they can be considered as one whole market set by long-term investors in terms of their portfolio diversification. On the other hand, if these markets turn out not to be cointegrated, they can still serve as good avenues for portfolio diversification. If there are leads and lags between these markets, the markets can offer arbitrage opportunities that can be exploited by investors. The results of this study can therefore be of practical significance to investors who are considering the ASEAN region for investment diversification.

The study finds that in the long-term, these markets are not significantly linked. However, in the short-term, with the exception of Indonesia, all the ASEAN markets have significant linkages with each other. Bidirectional linkages occur between any pair of markets for Malaysia, Singapore and Thailand. A unidirectional linkage exists between the Philippines and Singapore, with causality running from the former to the latter. Malaysia is the most influential market while Singapore and Thailand are the markets with most linkages with other markets. Indonesia is not linked at all with any other ASEAN market. Generally, each market responds to a shock from another market within a week, and the interaction continues, although at a much lower level, beyond two months.

The remaining parts of this chapter are organised as follows. The first section provides an institutional background of the ASEAN markets. This is followed by the results and the conclusion of the chapter.

Institutional Setting

Economic Interdependence Among ASEAN

There has been a growing economic interdependence among the ASEAN countries starting in the 1980s. The proportion of ASEAN exports going to ASEAN itself has risen from 18.2 per cent in 1980 to 19.6 per cent in 1990 (DFAT, 1992b). This is most pronounced in the case of Malaysia where over 30 per cent of its total exports went to ASEAN in 1989 (Ariff and Chye, 1992). Table 5.1 below provides further evidence on the growing economic linkages among the ASEAN nations. As can be seen in this table, intra-ASEAN trade between 1989 and 1994 has grown much faster than ASEAN's trade with other regions. Intra-industry trade in ASEAN has been growing due to the activities of multinationals (Ariff and Chye, 1992). This interdependence has been supported by the establishment of AFTA (ASEAN Free Trade Area) in 1992 which provided for the liberalisation of trade within ASEAN.

Table 5.1   ASEAN regional trade

Country or region	ASEAN exports to:			ASEAN imports from:		
	1989 ($USm)	1994 ($USm)	Trend growth (%)	1989 ($USm)	1994 ($USm)	Trend growth (%)
Brunei	584	1169	14.6	309	510	3.4
Indonesia	1672	2942	10.4	2618	5956	22.6
Malaysia	7027	21242	24.6	7899	20912	19.5
Philippine	1274	2794	19.8	584	1440	23.1
Singapore	8496	21250	18.7	6719	15161	13.5
Thailand	3667	8193	12.5	2263	6926	25.3
ASEAN	*22719*	*57590*	*19.0*	*20392*	*50905*	*18.4*
Australia	2767	4741	13.2	3565	6674	10.2
Canada	1118	2311	16.7	1319	1537	–1.3
Chile	84	195	22.2	276	516	14.0
China	2813	6554	26.0	3851	7226	9.8
Hong Kong	5293	15112	23.9	3299	7748	18.0
Japan	23194	36110	6.9	29918	68993	15.7
South Korea	3735	7606	11.1	3815	11811	22.3
Mexico	157	868	34.8	190	230	0.5
New Zealand	316	745	19.8	570	911	9.0
PNG	191	257	10.0	59	186	27.2
Taiwan	3005	9004	22.7	6417	12402	10.9
US	25976	51850	17.0	19624	39334	13.8
APEC	*91369*	*192983*	*15.8*	*93293*	*208473*	*15.4*
European Union	17377	37627	13.5	16930	40520	12.8
Other	12824	25894	15.9	15929	29388	8.9
Total	*121570*	*256504*	*15.5*	*126153*	*278381*	*14.3*

Source: Department of Foreign Affairs and Trade, *The APEC Region and Investment*, Australian Government Publishing Service, Canberra, 1994, p. 26 (as cited in p. 3 of Edwards and Wong, 1996).

Previous studies (e.g., Yan, 1986; Ariff and Chye, 1992) have found that there is a high degree of economic interaction between Malaysia and Singapore and this interaction between the two countries has served as the cornerstone of interdependence among the ASEAN markets. Another factor that is being cited for the increasing economic integration among the ASEAN countries is the existence of ethnic Chinese business networks in these countries (Edwards and Wong, 1996). Ethnic Chinese have a tendency to conduct inter-country trade.

Financial Deregulation in ASEAN

Each of the five ASEAN countries included in this study went through substantial financial deregulation in terms of the abolition of controls on interest rates, capital outflows and financial institution activities. The case of Singapore has been discussed in Chapter 4. Singapore had its financial deregulation as far back as the early 1970s and has since then maintained open and liberalised financial markets. The other ASEAN countries, however, have embarked on substantial deregulation only in the late 1980s although some of them had actually started to make some reforms as early as 1971 but these reforms were either stopped or were not sustained. Among these other ASEAN countries, Malaysia has been the most successful in terms of reforms in its financial system (Cole, 1995).

Malaysia had liberalised interest rates in 1978 but then reinstated them in 1983 due to financial market problems during that time. After stability had been restored, Malaysia resumed its reform and continued to do so. However, in the banking sector existing government regulations continue to have a bias towards government or Malay-owned banks. In the case of Indonesia, it actually eliminated foreign capital controls in 1971 but only lifted interest and credit controls in 1983 and removed most restrictions on bank activities in 1988.

The Philippines started easing its control on interest rates in 1980 but this stopped in 1981 and then continued with this reform again in 1986. Capital controls were only effectively abolished in 1993. Regulations on bank entry and the setting up of branches were relaxed in 1989 but there is still a prohibition on the entry of wholly-owned foreign banks and foreign ownership in joint ventures is limited to 40 per cent. Turning to the case of Thailand, this country reduced control over interest rates, capital controls and financial activities starting in 1990 (Cole, 1995). Commercial banks have been allowed to expand their activities into underwriting and funds management. However, there were still significant restrictions on entry of new banks and also loan allocation requirements are still in place (Cole, 1995 and White, 1995).

Rhee (1992) had classified Singapore as a "fully liberalised" market characterised by the absence of foreign exchange controls and the absence of prohibition on foreign ownership of domestic firms, except those which are considered to be vital to the national interest. The other four ASEAN markets were classified by Rhee as "substantially open but not liberalised". No significant foreign exchange controls exist in these markets but there are limitations to foreign ownership of domestic companies. Capital could therefore flow in and out of ASEAN.

Comparative Features of the ASEAN Stock Markets

In terms of capitalisation and turnover, it can be seen in Table 5.2 that the Malaysian equity market is the largest among the five ASEAN markets. This is followed by Singapore and Thailand, and then by the Philippines. The Indonesian market is the smallest among the group. Except for Malaysia which was ranked number 9 in the world in 1993, the other markets are relatively small as compared to other markets in the world. Table 5.2 further shows that the Malaysian stock market also has the highest number of listed companies with Thailand coming in second, and the Philippines third. Singapore, which is the second

Table 5.2   Characteristics of ASEAN markets, 1995

Characteristics	Malaysia	Singapore	Philippines	Indonesia	Thailand
Market capitalisation					
• *Value ($USbn)*	222.7	148.0	58.9	66.6	141.5
• *Rank*	12	18	26	25	20
Value traded					
• *Value ($USbn)*	76.8	60.5	14.7	14.4	57.0
• *Rank*	16	17	29	30	19
Listed companies					
• *Number*	529	212	205	238	347
• *Rank*	15	33	35	17	18
P/E ratio	25.1	25.8	19.0	19.8	21.7

Source: *Emerging Stock Markets Factbook*, 1994; Asiamoney, *The 1994 Guide to Asian Equities Market*

largest stock market in terms of capitalisation, has the second lowest number of listed companies. This could mean that Singaporean companies are bigger in size compared to those of Thailand and the Philippines. As can be seen also in Table 5.2, the Malaysian market also has the highest P/E ratio, followed by the Philippines closely. Indonesia is a far third, and then closely followed by Thailand and the Philippines.

In terms of capitalisation, the ASEAN equity markets have grown at very high rates. As can be seen in Table 5.3, the Indonesian market has registered the highest growth rate (33200 per cent) from 1989 to 1993. This is followed by Thailand (1508 per cent) and the Philippines (1270 per cent) and then by Malaysia (856 per cent) and Singapore (517 per cent).

The Indonesian stock market has grown fastest since 1989 in terms of turnover. This is followed by Malaysia. As can be seen in Table 5.4, in 1989, it was just third among the group but by 1993, it had become the largest in terms of turnover. Singapore was then the biggest followed by Thailand.

One important feature of ASEAN markets that should also be pointed out is the existence of price limits in Malaysia and Thailand, which are set, respectively, at 30 per cent and 10 per cent of the previous day's closing price (Naughton, 1999, p. 29). There are no price limits in the other ASEAN countries.

Table 5.3   ASEAN equity markets capitalisation, 1988–95 ($US billion)

Year	Malaysia	Singapore	Philippine	Indonesia	Thailand
1988	23.3	24.0	4.3	0.2	8.8
1989	39.8	35.9	12.0	2.2	25.6
1990	48.6	34.3	5.9	8.1	23.9
1991	58.6	47.6	10.2	6.8	35.8
1992	94.0	48.8	13.8	12.0	58.3
1993	220.3	132.7	40.3	33.0	130.5
1994	199.3	134.5	55.5	47.2	131.5
1995	222.7	148.0	58.9	66.6	141.5
Per cent change 1988–95	856	517	1270	33200	1508

Source: *Emerging Stock Markets Factbook*, 1998

Table 5.4   ASEAN equity markets value of trade, 1988–95 ($US billion)

Year	Malaysia	Singapore	Philippine	Indonesia	Thailand
1988	2.6	4.5	0.9	0.004	5.6
1989	6.9	13.7	2.4	0.5	13.4
1990	10.9	20.3	1.2	4.0	22.9
1991	10.6	18.1	1.5	2.9	30.1
1992	21.7	14.1	3.1	3.9	72.1
1993	153.7	81.6	6.8	9.2	86.9
1994	126.4	81.0	13.9	11.8	80.2
1995	76.8	60.5	14.7	14.4	57.0
Per cent change 1988–95	2854	1244	1533	3599	918

Source: *Emerging Stock Markets Factbook*, 1998

ASEAN markets are generally classified as "emerging markets". According to Brailsford and Heaney (1998), emerging markets are now generally classified into four groups. The first group consists of markets which are in their early stage of development and are generally characterised by a listing of a small number of shares, and low level of capitalisation and liquidity. The second group is comprised of markets which are larger, with greater liquidity and number of listings, and with some foreign equities. The third group consists of those markets which have started to mature.   These are markets with substantial capitalisation and with volatility which is not high.   The final group comprises of markets which are relatively liquid, high volume of trading, broad listing of securities, and volatilities which are close to those of developed markets.   Malaysia, Indonesia, the Philippines, and Thailand are classified with the second group while Singapore belongs to the fourth group.

Hypothesis Testing Results

This section applies the techniques of cointegration, Granger-causality, forecast variance decomposition and impulse response analyses to test the degree and structure of relationship among the ASEAN equity market prices using MSCI weekly data covering the period 1988–95. Because of the close economic linkage between these countries, and the fact that their equity markets are quite similar in size, it is expected that these markets will mutually affect each other significantly.

Unit Root Test Results

The results are given in Table 5.5. As can be seen for each market, the null hypothesis of the existence of unit roots was not rejected at the level form of the data but was accepted at the first-differenced form, by both the ADF and PP tests. Hence, it may be concluded that each data series is stationary and integrated of order 1 or I(1).

Optimum lag test results Some studies (Eun and Shim, 1989; Espitia and Santamaria, 1994) have found that information from one national market spill-over to other national markets within a period of one week. Hence, using Equation (3.16), lags of 1 versus 2 are first tested $\left(H_0:k = 1 \text{ versus } H_A:k = 2\right)$. If the null hypothesis is rejected, the test continues by testing the next higher lags. The results are presented in Table 5.6. These show that the highest number of lags that is significant at the 5 per cent level is 9. Thus, a lag of 9 is adopted as the optimal lag for the VAR model.

Table 5.5   Unit root test results — ASEAN
(H_0: unit root versus H_A: no unit root)

Market	ADF test results*		PP test results*	
	Level	First difference	Level	First difference
Malaysia	−2.52	−5.22	−2.24	−16.82
Singapore	−1.00	−5.02	−1.07	−17.42
Philippines	−0.91	−3.71	−0.80	−17.04
Indonesia	−0.36	−4.55	−0.45	−17.96
Thailand	−0.71	−6.12	−1.21	−20.07

* critical value (10 per cent level): −2.57

Table 5.6   Likelihood ratio test on lags — ASEAN

Lags	Likelihood ratio value	P-value
1 versus 2	40.96	0.02
2 versus 3	52.99	0.00
3 versus 4	47.34	0.00
4 versus 5	38.21	0.04
5 versus 6	42.87	0.01
6 versus 7	41.51	0.02
7 versus 8	42.05	0.02
8 versus 9	41.36	0.02
9 versus 10	29.14	0.26

Cointegration Test Results

Since the unit root test results show that each of the data series is $I(1)$, the cointegration test based on the Johansen (1998) procedure is conducted. Using Equation (3.18), the trace statistics are calculated to test the null hypothesis of $r = 0$ (no cointegration), versus the alternative hypothesis of $r > 0$ (cointegration). The computed trace statistic corresponding to $r = 0$ is 17.46. Since, the critical value of the trace statistic is 71.47, as shown in Table A.3, p. 209 of Johansen and Juselius (1990), the null hypothesis cannot be rejected. Thus, the ASEAN markets are not cointegrated. This means that there is no significant long-term price linkage among the ASEAN equity markets.

Granger-causality Test Results

Since no cointegration exists between the different time series the Granger-causality test was performed, based on Equations (3.19) and (3.20). Based on Equation (3.23), F-statistics are calculated to test the null hypothesis that X does not affect $Y(H_0:$all $b_j = 0)$ against the alternative hypothesis that $X \rightarrow Y(H_A:$at least one $b_j \neq 0)$. The null hypothesis that Y does not affect $X(H_0:$all $b_j^* = 0)$ versus the alternative hypothesis that $Y \rightarrow X(H_A:$at least one $b_j^* \neq 0)$ is also tested. The calculated F-statistics are presented in Table 5.7.

Table 5.7　Calculated F-statistics based on
equations (3.19) and (3.20) — ASEAN
(P-values in parenthesis)

Market explained	Explanatory markets				
	Malaysia	Singapore	Philippines	Indonesia	Thailand
Malaysia	1.81[b]	3.07[a]	4.06[a]	0.25	3.36[a]
	(0.06)	(0.00)	(0.00)	(0.99)	(0.00)
Singapore	2.67[a]	2.45[a]	2.87[a]	0.33	2.66[a]
	(0.01)	(0.01)	(0.00)	(0.96)	(0.01)
Philippines	1.94[a]	1.58	1.71[b]	0.39	4.37[a]
	(0.04)	(0.12)	(0.08)	(0.94)	(0.00)
Indonesia	0.80	0.69	1.01	3.41[a]	1.07
	(0.62)	(0.72)	(0.43)	(0.00)	(0.38)
Thailand	1.84[b]	2.10[a]	3.10[a]	0.40	1.10
	(0.06)	(0.03)	(0.00)	(0.93)	(0.36)

a significant at 5 per cent level
b significant at 10 per cent level

As shown, with the exception of Indonesia, all ASEAN equity
markets are significantly linked with each other. The Indonesian equity
market is only significantly linked with its own past prices but not with
those of other markets. Malaysia and Thailand have a bidirectional, or
two-way linkage, with all the other markets, except with Indonesia.
Singapore has a two-way causality with all the other markets except
Indonesia (where it has no linkage at all) and with the Philippines
(where it has a unidirectional causality running from the Philippines to
Singapore). The Philippines also has a two-way causality with each of
the other markets, except with Indonesia (no linkage) and with
Singapore (one way causality only). The unidirectional relationship
between the Philippines and Singapore is one where the Philippines
leads Singapore. This could be due to the fact that Singapore has
significant investments in the Philippines while the Philippines does not
have the same in Singapore and therefore any changes occurring in the
Philippines seem to affect the Singaporean market. Overall, these
results show clearly that in the short-run the four ASEAN markets of

Malaysia, Singapore, the Philippines and Thailand have close linkages, while Indonesia seems to be the exception.

Forecast Variance Decomposition Analyses Results

The forecast variance decomposition analysis shows the proportion of the changes in the price in a particular equity market arising out of random shocks that can be attributed to random shocks coming from each market. For example, this analysis states that the percentage of the changes in the price in Malaysia that is due to random shocks can be attributed to random shocks coming from itself, Singapore, the Philippines, Indonesia or Thailand. The results of this analysis are shown in Table 5.8.

The values shown diagonally in the table indicate the percentage of the forecast variance of a particular market that is due to random shocks coming from itself. The values for Malaysia, Singapore, the Philippines, Indonesia, and Thailand are 92.32, 46.35, 79.79, 84.67 and 58.88, respectively. Malaysia has the highest value. This means that it is the market that has the biggest domestic effect on its price. On the other hand, Singapore has the lowest value. This means that within the ASEAN market, it has the most international source of random shocks affecting its price. The biggest proportion of change in Singapore's price from random shocks is due to Malaysia (48.02 per cent). The change in Singapore's price resulting from random shocks is therefore primarily accounted for by Malaysia, in addition to itself. In the case of Malaysia, the main source is primarily itself since it accounts for 92.32 per cent of the change in price due to random shocks. For the Philippines, the

Table 5.8   Forecast variance decomposition analyses — ASEAN (4-week time forecasting horizon)

Forecast variance of:	Percentage of forecast variance due to:				
	Malaysia	Singapore	Philippines	Indonesia	Thailand
Malaysia	92.32	2.45	4.36	0.17	0.70
Singapore	48.02	46.35	3.90	0.42	1.30
Philippines	10.76	4.61	79.79	0.12	4.72
Indonesia	9.12	1.51	3.71	84.67	0.99
Thailand	29.40	5.45	5.81	0.45	58.88

foreign market with the largest influence is Malaysia (10.76 per cent). Thailand and Singapore account for 4.72 per cent and 4.61 per cent respectively, of the Philippines forecast variance, which may be considered relatively important. In the case of Indonesia, most of the changes are due to itself (84.67 per cent), with some significant influence coming from Malaysia (9.12 per cent). Thailand is heavily influenced by Malaysia (29.40 per cent) and also to a considerable extent by the Philippines (5.81 per cent) and Singapore (5.45 per cent). In summary, therefore, in terms of random shocks, Malaysia is primarily a market influenced by itself while Singapore is primarily influenced by Malaysia. The market with the biggest influence on the Philippines, Thailand and Indonesia is also Malaysia. Malaysia is also the most influential on Thailand, although the Philippines and Singapore also exert some significant influence. Thus, in terms of the forecast variance analyses results, it can be concluded that Malaysia is the most, and Indonesia is the least, influential among the ASEAN markets. Thailand is the market most affected by other ASEAN markets.

Impulse Response Analyses Results

Since Malaysia significantly affected all the other ASEAN markets, the manner of response to a Malaysian shock by Singapore, the Philippines, Indonesia and Thailand is investigated. This can be seen from the results of the impulse response analyses which are presented in Figure 5.1.

It can be seen that Singapore responds immediately to a Malaysian shock in a significant and positive manner during week 1. After week 1, Singapore continues to react to the Malaysian shock, even up to week 10, with negative responses in weeks 4 and 5, and then with positive responses starting in week 6. The Philippines, Indonesia and Thailand also respond positively to a Malaysian shock during week 1 but in a much more subdued manner. Except for week 5, the Philippine responses are all positive, continuing also even up to week 10.

Indonesia had the same pattern of response, more or less, except that the negative responses are registered during weeks 7 and 10. Except for week 4, Thailand's responses are also mostly positive.

Since Thailand and Singapore also influence the Philippines, it is useful to examine how the Philippines reacted to shocks coming from these two markets. This is done in Figure 5.2. As shown, the Philippines does not respond immediately to a Thai shock. It is not until week 2 that the Philippines makes a response, and this response is positive. The Philippine response continues until week 10, with negative responses in weeks 3, 5 and 6, and positive responses for all other weeks. In the case of a Singaporean shock, the Philippines responds immediately in week 1 and continues to do so until week 10, with positive responses from weeks 1 to 5 and negative ones after that.

Thailand, as mentioned earlier, is affected by the Philippines and Singapore, in addition to Malaysia. Thus, it is interesting to know Thailand's reaction to shocks from the Philippines and Singapore. This is done in Figure 5.3.

Thailand makes a positive and immediate response to a Philippines' shock in week 1, an even bigger positive response in week 2 and then a smaller positive response in week 3. Thereafter, alternating between

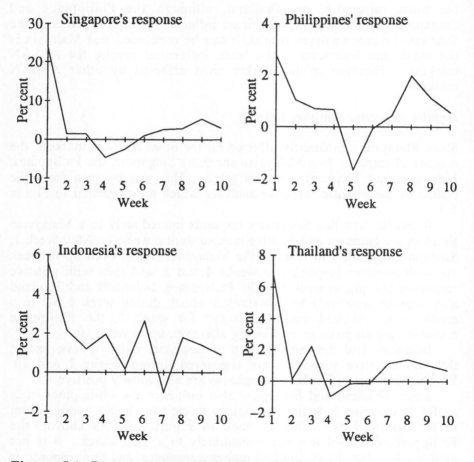

Figure 5.1 Response to a Malaysian shock

negative and positive responses occur from weeks 4 to 7, then by all negative responses in weeks 8, 9 and 10. Thailand makes a strong immediate positive response to a Singaporean shock in week 1 followed by much smaller positive responses in weeks 2, 3 and 4. Negative responses are then made in weeks 6 and 7 followed by positive responses in weeks 8 and 9 and a negative response in week 10.

Thus, overall, the results of the impulse response analyses show that the interaction among the ASEAN markets occurs immediately and continues even beyond two months.

Conclusion

This chapter investigates the extent and structure of price linkages among five ASEAN markets (Malaysia, Singapore, Philippines, Indonesia and Thailand) both in the long-run and in the short-run. No cointegration was found among the markets as a group. Thus, there is no significant long-term price linkage among the ASEAN equity

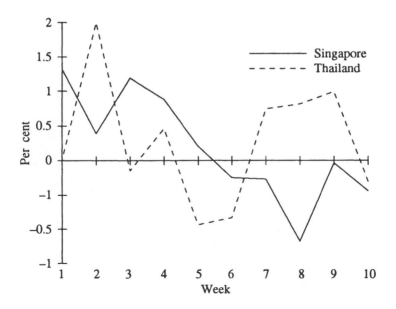

Figure 5.2 Philippine response to a Thailand and Singapore shock

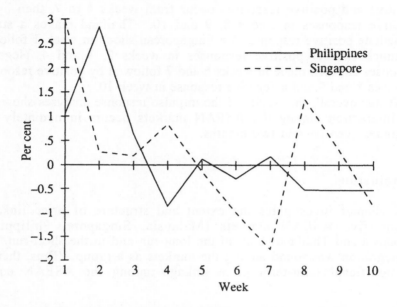

Figure 5.3 Thailand response to a Philippine and Singapore shock

markets. In the short-term, the results of the Granger-causality test reveal however that these markets are all significantly linked with each other. There is a bidirectional causality between Malaysia and Singapore, Singapore and Thailand, and Malaysia and Thailand. On the other hand, a unidirectional causality occurs between the Philippines and Singapore with causality running from the former to the latter. The forecast variance decomposition analyses show that Malaysia is the most, and Indonesia, is the least influential among the ASEAN markets. Finally, the results of the impulse response analyses indicate that the interaction among the ASEAN markets occurs immediately and continues even beyond two months. Thus, the ASEAN markets can serve as good avenues for long-term portfolio diversification. In the short-term, these markets offer opportunities for arbitrage profits because of the existence of leads and lags.

6 Equity Market Price Interdependence between Australia and ASEAN

Introduction

This chapter investigates the extent and structure of equity market price linkages between Australia and five Association of Southeast Asian Nations (ASEAN) countries (Malaysia, Singapore, Philippines, Indonesia and Thailand), both in the long-run and in the short-run using cointegration based on the Johansen (1988) procedure, Granger-causality, forecast variance decomposition and impulse response analyses. Given ASEAN's economic success, Australian investors are being encouraged to consider ASEAN as a venue for possible portfolio diversification (DFAT, 1992b). It is therefore important that the degree and nature of linkages between the financial markets of Australia and ASEAN be assessed and fully understood. This information is presently unavailable. The Reserve Bank of Australia has claimed that Australia's economic cycle now seems to be linked with that of Asia (The Australian, 21 August 1997). This seems to imply that Australian financial markets may also be integrated with those of Asia, including ASEAN. The recent crisis which has seen sudden currency depreciation in ASEAN countries, with Thailand, the Philippines, Indonesia and Malaysia being significantly affected,[1] has raised concerns in Australia that ASEAN financial market problems may be transmitted to Australia. Thus, it is important, that the degree and nature of interdependence between Australian and ASEAN's financial markets be investigated.

Studies on Australia's equity market linkages with other countries are relatively few and have mostly been focused on developed markets. The few studies regarding Australia's linkage with Asia have mostly been with Japan and the so-called East Asian Tigers — Taiwan, Hong Kong, Singapore and Korea (see, for instance, Kwan, et al., 1996; Allen and MacDonald, 1995). Neither do these studies (except Allen and MacDonald, 1995) provide a comprehensive investigation of equity market integration, either in the short-term or in the long-term. Most studies assess only the extent or degree of integration, but the structure of integration has never been explored. This study seeks to redress this deficiency and to provide new, robust and more comprehensive evidence on the equity market integration between Australia and ASEAN.

If the ASEAN markets are found to be cointegrated with Australia, then these markets cannot serve as good avenues for portfolio diversification among Australian investors. If there are leads and lags between Australia and the ASEAN markets, then there are arbitrage opportunities that Australian investors can exploit. The results of this study can therefore be of practical significance to Australian investors who are considering the ASEAN region for investment diversification.

The remaining part of this chapter is organised as follows. The first section presents the institutional context of the study. The following section discusses the empirical results and the final section concludes the chapter.

Institutional Setting

Trade

ASEAN is a significant trade partner of Australia, both in exports and imports. As can be seen in Table 6.1, Singapore, Indonesia, Malaysia, Thailand and the Philippines accounted for 12.6 per cent of total

Table 6.1   Australia's trade with Southeast Asia, 1998

	Merchandise exports			Merchandise imports		
	$A'000	% share	Rank	$A'000	% share	Rank
Singapore	3696636	4.2	8	2641118	2.9	10
Indonesia	2750690	3.1	10	2868372	3.2	8
Malaysia	2097262	2.4	11	2404464	2.7	12
Thailand	1389811	1.6	14	1474526	1.6	15
Philippine	1165419	1.3	17	418287	0.5	31
Vietnam	324483	0.4	32	663,961	0.7	25
Brunei	52112	0.06	63	–	–	–
Cambodia	10027	0.00	101	863	0.00	120
Laos	1946	0.00	152	–	–	–

Source: DFAT (1998), *Composition of Trade*

Australian exports. This group also accounted for about 10.9 per cent of total Australian imports. These countries are among Australia's top 20 trade partners. In fact, in terms of exports, Singapore and Indonesia were among the top 10, with Singapore ranked 8 and Indonesia ranked 10.

During the period covered by this study, ASEAN's importance as an export market for Australia has increased. As shown in Table 6.2, ASEAN's share of total Australian exports has increased from 7.2 per cent in 1988 to about 15.2 per cent in 1995. The biggest increase was registered by Singapore which went up from 2.8 per cent to 5.4 per cent. This was followed by Indonesia which recorded an increase from 1.4 per cent to 3.1 per cent, and then by the Philippines which went up from 0.6 per cent to 1.2 per cent and by Thailand which increased from 0.8 per cent to 2.3 per cent. Malaysia's share also went up from 1.6 per cent to 3.0 per cent.

As a source of imports for Australia, ASEAN has also increased in importance over the period covered by this study. As can be seen in Table 6.3, ASEAN's share of Australia's imports increased from 6.3 per cent in 1988 to 8.2 per cent in 1995. The biggest increase came from Singapore (from 2.2 per cent to 3.0 per cent). This was followed by Thailand, Malaysia and then Indonesia. The Philippine's share of Australia's imports, however, remained constant at 0.3 per cent.

Table 6.2   Australian merchandise exports to Southeast Asia, 1988–95

	1988		1995	
	$A million	% share	$A million	% share
Singapore	1166	2.8	3639	5.4
Malaysia	655	1.6	2041	3.0
Thailand	317	0.8	1558	2.3
Indonesia	595	1.4	2105	3.1
Philippines	268	0.6	839	1.2
ASEAN (5)*	3001	7.2	10182	15.2
World	41409	100.0	67063	100.0

* Total for Singapore, Malaysia, Thailand, Indonesia and the Philippines.

Source: DFAT, *Composition of Trade; Direction of Trade*, various years

Table 6.3 Australian merchandise imports from Southeast Asia, 1980–98

	1988		1995	
	$A million	% share	$A million	% share
Singapore	898	2.2	2247	3.0
Malaysia	609	1.5	1421	1.9
Thailand	331	0.8	970	1.3
Indonesia	588	1.4	1198	1.6
Philippines	127	0.3	259	0.3
ASEAN (5)*	2553	6.3	6095	8.2
World	40591	100.0	74634	100.0

* Total for Singapore, Malaysia, Thailand, Indonesia and the Philippines.

Source: DFAT, *Composition of Trade; Direction of Trade*, various years

Investment

Australia's investment in ASEAN has been relatively insignificant since the mid 1980s. The same is true with ASEAN's investment in Australia (DFAT, 1992b). Hence, the main economic linkage between Australia and ASEAN has been in the trade area. Australia's investment overseas has been mainly in the US, UK and New Zealand. As shown in Table 6.4, in 1995, only 5.4 per cent of Australia's total investment was in ASEAN while 28 per cent was in the US, and 17.2 per cent was in the UK.

ASEAN's investment in Australia has also been relatively insignificant. The main investors in Australia have been the US, the UK, and Japan (DFAT, 1992b). In 1995, as shown in Table 6.5, ASEAN accounted for a meagre 2.17 percent of total foreign investment in Australia.

Comparative Features of Australian and ASEAN Equity Markets

In terms of capitalisation, the Australian equity market, although somewhat larger, is comparable to that of Malaysia, as shown in Table 6.6. It is bigger than Singapore, the Philippines, Indonesia or Thailand. The Australian stock market ranked number 11 in comparison to a rank of 12 for Malaysia. In terms of value traded, Australia was well ahead of Malaysia with Australia having a rank of 12 while Malaysia was further down at rank number 16.

It can also be seen in Table 6.6 that the Australian equity market has more companies listed than any of the ASEAN markets. In fact, in 1995, in terms of this aspect, Australia was ranked number 7 in the world, Thailand number 18, Indonesia number 17, Singapore number 33, and the Philippines number 35. Table 6.6 also shows that Australia has a P/E ratio that is close to those of Thailand, Indonesia and the Philippines and relatively lower than those of Malaysia and Singapore.

The ASEAN stock markets have grown very much faster than the Australian equity market during the period of this study. As shown in Table 6.7, over the period 1988 to 1995, the Australian stock market grew by only around 78 per cent as compared to Indonesia's 33,200 per cent; Thailand's 1508 per cent; the Philippines' 1270 per cent; Malaysia's 856 per cent; and Singapore's 517 per cent.

Table 6.4 **Level of Australian investment in ASEAN and other selected countries, 1988–95**

	1988 $A million	% share	1995 $A million	% share	1988–95 % change
Singapore	1090	1.5	4895	3.1	349
Malaysia	170	0.2	2104	1.3	1138
Thailand	93	0.1	986	0.6	960
Indonesia	29	0.03	169	0.1	483
Philippines	46	0.06	391	0.2	750
ASEAN (5)*	1275	1.7	8545	5.4	570
US	20808	27.9	44777	28.1	115
UK	–	–	27507	17.2	–
Japan	3321	4.4	9365	5.9	182
World	74619	100.0	159552	100.0	114

* Total for Singapore, Malaysia, Thailand, Indonesia and the Philippines.

Source: DFAT (1995), *The APEC Region: Trade and Investment*, ABS (1998), *Foreign Investment Position, Australia*

Table 6.5   Investment in Australia by ASEAN and other selected countries, 1988–95

	1988 $A million	1988 % share	1995 $A million	1995 % share	1988–95 % change
Singapore	6923	3.4	7695	1.8	11
Malaysia	376	0.2	872	0.2	132
Thailand	60	0.03	299	0.1	398
Indonesia	18	0.00	115	0.03	539
Philippines	3	0.00	215	0.05	7067
ASEAN (5)*	7380	3.7	9196	2.17	25
USA	40572	20.2	91724	21.7	126
UK	–	–	76983	18.2	–
Japan	29849	14.9	51116	12.1	71
World	200792	100.0	422750	100.0	110

* Total for Singapore, Malaysia, Thailand, Indonesia and the Philippines.

Source: DFAT (1995), *The APEC Region: Trade and Investment*, ABS (1998), *Foreign Investment Position, Australia*

Table 6.6   Performance characteristics of Australia and ASEAN markets, 1995

Characteristics	Malaysia	Singapore	Philippines	Indonesia	Thailand	Australia
Market capitalisation						
• *Value (\$USbn)*	222.7	148.0	58.9	66.6	141.5	245.2
• *Rank*	12	18	26	25	20	11
Value traded						
• *Value (\$USbn)*	76.8	60.5	14.7	14.4	57.0	98.6
• *Rank*	16	17	29	30	19	12
Listed companies						
• *Number*	529	212	205	238	347	1178
• *Rank*	15	33	35	17	18	7
P/E ratio	25.1	25.8	19.0	19.8	21.7	21.5

Source: *Emerging Stock Markets Factbook*, 1994; Asiamoney, *The 1994 Guide to Asian Equities Market*

Table 6.7   Australia and ASEAN equity markets capitalisation, 1988–95 ($US billion)

Year	Australia	Malaysia	Singapore	Philippine	Indonesia	Thailand
1988	138.2	23.3	24.0	4.3	0.2	8.8
1989	141.0	39.8	35.9	12.0	2.2	25.6
1990	107.6	48.6	34.3	5.9	8.1	23.9
1991	144.9	58.6	47.6	10.2	6.8	35.8
1992	135.4	94.0	48.8	13.8	12.0	58.3
1993	204.0	220.3	132.7	40.3	33.0	130.5
1994	219.2	199.3	134.5	55.5	47.2	131.5
1995	245.2	222.7	148.0	58.9	66.6	141.5
% change 1988–95	77.4	856	517	1270	33200	1508

Source: *Emerging Stock Markets Factbook*, 1998

In terms of value traded, as can be seen in Table 6.8, the same picture emerges. The ASEAN equity markets had also grown very much faster than the Australian equity market. Indonesia had registered the fastest growth at 3,599 per cent followed by Malaysia (2,854 per cent), the Philippines (1,533 per cent), Singapore (1,244 per cent) and Thailand (918 per cent).

Table 6.8   Australia and ASEAN equity markets value of trade, 1988–95 ($US billion)

Year	Australia	Malaysia	Singapore	Philippine	Indonesia	Thailand
1988	37.4	2.6	4.5	0.9	0.004	5.6
1989	44.8	6.9	13 .7	2.4	0.5	13.4
1990	39.3	10.9	20.3	1.2	4.0	22.9
1991	46.8	10.6	18.1	1.5	2.9	30.1
1992	45.8	21.7	14.1	3.1	3.9	72.1
1993	67.7	153.7	81.6	6.8	9.2	86.9
1994	94.7	126.4	81.0	13.9	11.8	80.2
1995	98.6	76.8	60.5	14.7	14.4	57.0
% change 1988–95	164	2854	1244	1533	3599	918

Source: *Emerging Stock Markets Factbook*, 1998

Hypothesis Testing Results

Cointegration, Granger-causality, forecast variance decomposition and impulse response analyses were conducted using MSCI weekly data covering the period 1/1/88 to 8/12/95 to examine the price interdependence between Australia and ASEAN. Given the significant trade interaction between Australia and ASEAN since 1980 (DFAT, 1992b), and the significant financial deregulation which has occurred in each of these markets, it is expected that Australia will be cointegrated with ASEAN. Given also that Malaysia and Singapore are the dominant stock markets in ASEAN, it is expected that Australia will be significantly linked to them. Because these markets lie within the same time zone, it is also expected that Australia will respond immediately to any shocks coming from ASEAN within a week's time and ASEAN is expected to do the same with regards to shocks coming from Australia.

Unit Root Test Results

As can be seen in Table 6.9, both the ADF and PP test results show that all price series are not significant in their level forms but are significant in their first differenced form. This means that each data series is integrated of order 1 or I(1).

Optimum Lag Test Results

The results of the likelihood ratio test based on Equation (3.16) are presented in Table 6.10. As shown, the highest number of lags that is significant is 4 at the 5 per cent level and 9 at the 10 per cent level. In order to reduce the possibility of serial correlation, the higher lag of 9 is adopted for the VAR model.

Cointegration Test Results

Since all data series have been shown to be I(1), the cointegration test based on the Johansen (1988) procedure is conducted. The results are given in Table 6.11. As shown, $H_0: r = 0$ is rejected while $H_A: r \leq 1$ is accepted at both the 5 per cent and 10 per cent level of significance, and hence, there is one cointegrating vector that is significant. This means that Australia and ASEAN are cointegrated and are therefore significantly linked in the long-run.

Table 6.9 **Unit root test results — Australia and ASEAN**
(H_0: unit root versus H_A: no unit root)

Market	ADF test results*		PP test results*	
	Level	First difference	Level	First difference
Australia	−1.72	−4.76	−1.71	−20.72
Malaysia	−2.52	−5.22	−2.24	−16.82
Singapore	−1.00	−5.02	−1.07	−17.42
Philippines	−0.91	−3.71	−0.80	−17.04
Indonesia	−0.36	−4.55	−0.45	−17.96
Thailand	−0.71	−6.12	−1.21	−20.07

* critical value (10 per cent level): −2.57

Table 6.10 **Likelihood ratio test on lags — Australia and ASEAN**

Lags	Likelihood ratio value	P-value
1 versus 2	63.52	0.00
2 versus 3	57.81	0.01
3 versus 4	59.95	0.01
4 versus 5	48.28	0.08
5 versus 6	48.58	0.08
6 versus 7	49.18	0.07
7 versus 8	55.73	0.02
8 versus 9	50.79	0.05
9 versus 10	42.68	0.21

Table 6.11 Computed trace values — Australia and ASEAN

H_0	H_A	Computed trace value	Critical trace value*	
			0.10 level	0.05 level
$r = 0$	$r > 0$	99.55	89.48	94.15
$r \leq 1$	$r > 1$	61.63	64.84	68.52

* taken from Table 1, p. 467, of Osterwald-Lenum (1992)

Granger-causality Test Results

Since the different series are cointegrated, the Granger-causality test was performed based on Equations (3.21) and (3.22). Based on Equation (3.23), F-statistics are calculated to test the null hypothesis that X does not affect $Y(H_0$:all $b_j = 0$ and $\phi = 0)$ against the alternative hypothesis that X→Y$(H_A$:at least one $b_j \neq 0$ and/or $\phi \neq 0)$.   The null hypothesis that Y does not affect $X(H_0$:all $b_j^* = 0$ and $\phi^* = 0)$ versus the alternative hypothesis that Y→X$(H_A$:at least one $b_j^* \neq 0$ and/or $\phi \neq 0)$ is also tested. The calculated F-statistics are presented in Table 6.12.

Australia is significantly affected by Malaysia, Singapore, and Thailand, as can be seen in the second column of Table 6.12. On the other hand, as shown in column 3 of the same Table, Australia does not significantly affect any of the other markets. Malaysia, however, responds to changes in the other markets, including Australia, through the ECM variable which is found to be significant (see the last column of Table 6.12).

Forecast Variance Decomposition Analyses Results

The results of the forecast variance decomposition analyses are shown in Table 6.13. Random shocks from Australia have relatively little effect on the ASEAN markets. These markets are affected much more by random shocks coming from themselves. This is shown in Table 6.13 by the numbers in the Australia column which are much lower than those of Malaysia, Singapore, Thailand and the Philippines columns. Looking at the last row of Table 6.13, it can be seen that random shocks from Singapore have the highest effect on Australia. This is

Table 6.12 Calculated F-statistics based on equations (3.21) and (3.22) — Australia and ASEAN (P-value in parenthesis)

Market (1)	Effect on Australia (2)	Effect of Australia (3)	Effect of ECM (4)
Malaysia	2.85 (0.004)[a]	1.00 (0.432)	16.82 (0.000)[a]
Singapore	1.74 (0.089)[b]	0.94 (0.487)	0.73 (0.480)
Philippines	0.78 (0.620)	1.70 (0.095)	0.87 (0.420)
Indonesia	0.83 (0.578)	0.84 (0.571)	0.55 (0.580)
Thailand	2.04 (0.041)[a]	0.47 (0.875)	0.21 (0.810)
ECM	0.00 (0.999)		

a significant at the 5 per cent level
b significant at the 10 per cent level

followed by those from Malaysia, although on a much lower scale. Hence, the Australian market is most affected by random shocks coming from Singapore, Malaysia and Thailand.

Table 6.13 Forecast variance decomposition analyses — Australia and ASEAN (4-week time forecasting horizon)

Forecast variance of:	Percentage of forecast variance due to:					
	Malaysia	Singapore	Philippines	Indonesia	Thailand	Australia
Malaysia	92.32	2.45	4.36	0.17	0.70	1.45
Singapore	48.02	46.35	3.90	0.42	1.30	1.16
Philippines	10.76	4.61	79.79	0.12	4.72	2.61
Indonesia	9.12	1.51	3.71	84.67	0.99	0.97
Thailand	29.40	5.45	5.81	0.45	58.88	1.06
Australia	2.97	6.26	0.73	0.73	1.07	88.24

Impulse Response Analyses Results

As mentioned earlier, Australia is most significantly affected by random shocks from Malaysia, Singapore, and Thailand. The manner of Australia's response to these markets is therefore further investigated using the results from the impulse response analyses. These results are presented in Figure 6.1.

Australia immediately responds, positively, to a Malaysian shock on week 1. Australia's response continues even up to week 10 in a fluctuating manner with negative responses on weeks 2, 3 and 4, then a positive response on week 5, followed again by a negative response on week 6, positive responses on weeks 7 and 8, and so on. Australia responds to a Singapore shock also in a fluctuating manner that goes on from week 1 until week 10. During weeks 1 and 2, Australia's response

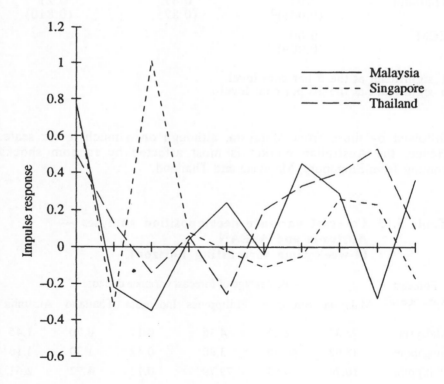

Figure 6.1 Australia's response to a Malaysia, Singapore and Thailand shock

to a Singapore shock is the same as its response to a Malaysian shock. However, for the other weeks, Australia's response to a Singapore shock is mostly opposite to that of its response to Malaysia. In the case of shocks from Thailand, Australia also immediately reacts with positive responses on weeks 1 and 2 and then followed by alternating responses on weeks 3, 4 and 5. Australia's reaction continues even beyond week 6, with positive responses.

Conclusion

Australia and ASEAN are found to be cointegrated and hence are significantly related in the long-term. The Granger-causality, forecast variance decomposition and impulse response analyses reveal that in the short-term, Australia is significantly influenced by Malaysia, Singapore and Thailand. Australia responds to shocks coming from these markets immediately on week 1 and continues its response up to week 10. The Australian equity market is not linked at all, in the short-term, with the Philippines and Indonesian stock markets. Thus, ASEAN does not provide portfolio diversification benefits to long-term Australian investors but in the short-term, the Philippines and Indonesia do.

Note

1   Just recently, the currencies of Thailand, the Philippines, Indonesia and Malaysia have suffered significant declines in values, especially the Thai baht which lost about 25 per cent of its value. These countries have blamed the action of speculators, particularly hedge funds, for this problem. As a consequence of this, Thailand has requested financial assistance from the International Monetary Fund (IMF). The IMF, in turn, has requested Australia's involvement in providing an emergency loan to Thailand. Furthermore, the ASEAN countries have explored the possibility of creating a fund that will be used to assist any ASEAN country that suddenly has a problem defending its currency. Japan has also been approached for help. Another major consequence of this crisis is that Indonesia has fully floated its currency.

7 Investigation of Equity Markets Interdependence Allowing for Autoregressive Conditional Heteroskedasticity (ARCH) Effects

Introduction

In the investigation of the interaction between the equity markets of Australia and its major trading partners which was conducted in Chapter 4, it was found that in the short-run, Australia is significantly influenced by the US and the UK and that Australia significantly affects the Hong Kong market. As found in Chapter 6, Australia is also significantly affected by Malaysia, Singapore and Thailand in the short run. In the case of ASEAN (see Chapter 5), it was shown that, with the exception of Indonesia, all of the ASEAN markets are linked with each other and Malaysia is the dominant market. This chapter investigates whether these results pertaining to the short-term interaction between markets are further supported when ARCH effects are taken into account. Thus, the results obtained from this chapter provide an indication as to which ones of these earlier results can be accepted with a high degree of confidence. However, even if any earlier finding does not find support from the results in this chapter, this earlier finding remains acceptable pending further investigation in the future based on VAR ARCH-based models that allow for cross-market effects in the variance equations.

Standard generalised ARCH or GARCH and exponential GARCH or EGARCH models are applied to take into account ARCH effects in the data. These models have been shown to perform well in capturing the short-term dynamics of share price behaviour (Ng, et al., 1991). Since multivariate models are recognised to have more advantages over the univariate ones, an attempt was made to fit multivariate VAR-GARCH and VAR-EGARCH models which are multivariate simultaneous equation models. Unfortunately, with these models, no convergence in the calculations could be achieved due to the great number of parameters that have to be estimated within a nonlinear maximisation context. Hence, this chapter had to settle with the use of univariate GARCH and EGARCH models. The results of the investigation provide further support to the study's earlier finding that the UK and US are influential on Australia.

It is already well-accepted in the finance literature that heteroskedasticity is a characteristic of financial time series data. For a certain period of time, volatilities can be successively large and in another period of time, these can be successively low. This volatility clustering could be due to the sensitivity of financial markets to such facts as "rumours, political upheavals, changes in government monetary and fiscal policies, and the like" (Gujarati, 1995) and indicates that there is some kind of autocorrelation in the variance of the error terms as volatility is not constant but varies from period to period (Gujarati, 1995; and Davidson and Mackinnon, 1993). This autocorrelation may be due to an autoregressive conditional heteroskedasticity (ARCH) effect rather than to serial correlation per se. In this situation, even if the error terms are not actually correlated but because their variance depends on past squared errors, this gives the impression that they are autocorrelated (Maddala, 1992, p. 264). The Durbin-Watson d-statistic will thus show serial correlation even if this is not the case. Diebold (1988) and Baillie and Bollerslev (1989) have shown that ARCH effects are often present in high frequency financial time series data such as daily and weekly stock market data and tend to occur less as the frequency of the data becomes lower.

The presence of ARCH characteristics affect· the correlation structure among the time series. Often, the calculation of pairwise correlations is based on the assumption that the time series involved are mean and variance stationary in which the conditional and unconditional estimates are the same. If, however, this assumption is not true as in the case where ARCH effects are present, the computed correlations will be greater than what they should actually be. In the area of finance, this has far-reaching significance as hedging and diversification strategies are based on knowledge of the correlation between different markets or assets. If correlations are overestimated in comparison to what they should be, this leads to underestimation of diversification benefits and will in turn lead to erroneous portfolio construction strategies.

The conditional (short-run) variance is easily shown to be smaller than the unconditional (long-run) variance (see Enders, 1995, pp. 141–

142; and Cuthberson, 1996, pp. 423–427). Therefore, the conditional variance is far more superior than the unconditional variance and this has given conditional variance modelling prominence in the finance literature (Bollerslev, et al., 1992). Different ways have been devised in modelling conditional variances in financial time series. One successful method has been the use of autoregressive conditional heteroskedasticity (ARCH)-based models which simultaneously model the conditional mean and conditional variance of a series. These models, which are based on the original work of Engle (1982) and generalised by Bollerslev (1986), have been shown to effectively capture the volatility clustering in financial data. Although other techniques for modelling time-varying volatilities have also been developed, ARCH remains unique in its balance between flexibility and tractability in modelling the short-term dynamics of stock return and volatility (Ng, et al., 1991; Hamao, et al., 1990). As an evidence of the widespread use of ARCH-based models, the survey by Bollerslev, et al. (1992) lists over two hundred papers in the finance literature that have applied ARCH-based models in the analysis of the behaviour of different types of financial assets in different financial markets.

In the context of the Australian equity market linkage with other countries, the present writer is only aware of one study based on ARCH methods which has examined interaction across markets — that of McNelis (1993). This study examines the relationship between the volatility in stock market returns between Australia and the countries of Germany, Japan (Nikkei), Singapore, the UK (Financial Times) and the US (Dow Jones) using monthly data from 1982 to 1992. Volatility is measured in terms of the Schwert (1989) index which is a two-step least-squares "short-cut" for the Bollerslev (1986) GARCH maximum likelihood estimation of the volatilities or conditional variances of the stock prices. It found that "Australia stock market volatility is closely linked with volatility in the UK market". The Nikkei and Dow Jones are also significant explanators of the Australian stock price volatility. Information on the volatility of the Australian index does not help to predict the volatility of the five other stock price indices. Information on the Australian stock index volatility only helps in the prediction of the Australian stock index itself. In terms of investigating equity market integration among ASEAN, the present writer is unaware of any scholarly study which has been conducted based on the ARCH methodology.

This chapter examines first moment linkages among the three groups of markets being considered in this book allowing for conditional heteroskedastic forecast error variances. It tests whether there are significant spill-overs in conditional mean across markets using standard

GARCH and exponential GARCH (or EGARCH) models for conditional heteroskedasticity. As will be explained later, the standard GARCH model posits a symmetric impact of news on volatility while the EGARCH allows for an asymmetric impact.

The remaining parts of this chapter are organised as follows. A background and discussion of the technical aspects — in terms of form, estimation and testing of the ARCH-based models used in this study. This is followed by a brief review of the major literature on equity market integration that use ARCH-based methodology. The remainder of the chapter presents the empirical results and the conclusion.

ARCH and GARCH Models

Standard ARCH and GARCH Models

Engle (1982) originally proposed the concept of ARCH in which the basic idea is that the variance of the error term at time t depends on the size of the squared error terms in previous periods (Davidson and Mackinnon, 1993). He suggests that the conditional variance or predictable volatility is dependent on past news: the older the news, the less effect it has on current volatility. In an ARCH(q) model, old news which arrived at the market more than q periods ago has no effect at all on current volatility (Engle and Ng, 1993). Engle (1982) therefore suggests that the conditional variance h_t can be modelled as a function of the lagged ε s in the form of a qth order autoregressive conditional heteroskedasticity model, ARCH (q) given below (Engle and Ng, 1993, p. 1751).

$$h_t = \alpha_0 + \sum_{i=1}^{q} \alpha_i \varepsilon_{t-i}^2$$

where $\alpha_0, \alpha_1, ...,$ and α_q are constant parameters. The effect of a shock i periods ago $\left(i \leq q\right)$ on current volatility is governed by the parameter α_i. Normally, it would be expected that $\alpha_i < \alpha_j$ for $i > j$.

Bollerslev (1986) generalises the ARCH (q) model to the GARCH (p,q) model. The GARCH model allows for both autoregressive and moving average components in the heteroskedastic variance (Enders, 1995, p. 147). The GARCH model is an infinite order ARCH model

(Engle and Ng, 1993). The GARCH (p,q) model can be expressed as follows (Engle and Ng, 1993, p. 1752):

$$h_t = \alpha_0 + \sum_{i=1}^{q} \alpha_i \varepsilon_{t-i}^2 + \sum_{i=1}^{p} \beta_i h_{t-i}$$

where $\alpha_1,...,\alpha_p,\beta_1,...,\beta_p$ are constant parameters.

The GARCH process assumes constant unconditional mean and variance, but the conditional mean and variance are time dependent. The time dependency in the conditional variance is meant to capture the clumping of volatility within time periods.

Within the finance literature, ε_t is a collective measure of news at time t. "A positive ε_t (an unexpected increase in price) suggests the arrival of good news, while a negative ε_t (an unexpected decrease in price) suggests the arrival of bad news. Further, a large value of $|\varepsilon_t|$ implies that the news is 'significant' or 'big' in the sense that it produces a large unexpected change in price." This can be seen in the following (Engle and Ng, 1993, p. 1751): "Let y_t be the rate of return of a particular stock or the market portfolio from $t-1$ to t. Also, let F_{t-1} be the past information set containing the realised values of all relevant variables up to time $t-1$. Since investors know the information in F_{t-1} when they make their investment decision at time $t-1$, the relevant expected return and volatility to the investors are the conditional expected value of y_t, given F_{t-1}, and the conditional variance of y_t, given F_{t-1}. Denote these by m_t and h_t, respectively, that is, $m_t \equiv E\left(y_t|F_{t-1}\right)$ and $h_t \equiv Var\left(y_t|F_{t-1}\right)$. Given these definitions, the unexpected return at time t is $\varepsilon_t \equiv y_t - m_t$ and ε_t is a collective measure of news at time t."

In the standard ARCH (q) and GARCH(p,q) model, the conditional variance depends only on the magnitude and not on the sign of the past news — that is, good news and bad news have the same impact on volatility. These models assume a symmetrical news impact on volatility. These models, therefore, would not be able to deal with a situation where an unexpected drop in price (bad news) increases predictable volatility more than an unexpected increase in price (good news) of similar magnitude.

Asymmetric Models

The asymmetry in news impact is well-supported by many studies within the finance literature (Black, 1976; Christie, 1982; French, et al., 1987; Nelson, 1991; and Schwert, 1990; among others). This phenomenon is usually explained in terms of the so-called "leverage effect". An unexpected decrease in share price decreases the value of equity relative to debt, and thus increases corporate leverage which in turn increases the risk of holding shares. This increase in risk translates into a rise in expected returns which further decreases the price of the share. Because of the leverage effect, bad news (a sudden decrease in share price) leads to a more magnified impact on volatility (a further decline in the share price). Some researchers, however, believe that the "leverage effect" may not be the only explanation for the asymmetric impact of news on volatility (French, et al., 1987). For instance, Campbell and Hentschel (1992) claim that the mere arrival of information itself could cause this asymmetry. News, per se, because of its being unexpected, will increase volatility. When news is bad, volatility increases more because it reinforces the initial increase in volatility arising from the surprise; however, when news is good, this tends to offset the initial impact of news on volatility which therefore leads to lower volatility.

In the field of finance, the use of a symmetric model when in fact an asymmetric model is called for creates serious consequences. In this situation, the model underestimates the impact of negative news and overestimates that of positive news. Thus, predictable volatility, which is an important input into the calculation of option prices and market risk premium, is either overestimated or underestimated. This can lead to serious errors in portfolio selection and hedging strategies.

Several GARCH models that allow for asymmetric impact have been developed. This chapter discusses only two of the most highly used asymmetric GARCH models — the exponential GARCH (EGARCH) model (Pagan and Schwert, 1990; and Nelson, 1991) and the GJR-GARCH model (Glosten, et al., 1993). The interested reader is referred to the survey by Bollerslev, et al. (1992) for a discussion of the other models.

The EGARCH Model

One of the earlier models that attempts to capture the asymmetry phenomenon is the EGARCH model which was first proposed by Pagan and Schwert (1990) and Nelson (1991). The form of the conditional variance equation of this model can be expressed using Nicholls and Tonuri's (1995) formulation as follows:

$$\log h_t = \alpha_0 + \sum_{i=1}^{q} \alpha_i f(z_{t-i}) + \sum_{j=1}^{p} \beta_i \log h_{t-j}$$

where $f(z_t) = \phi z_t + \gamma\left[|z_t| - E(|z_t|)\right]$

with the standardised residual $z_t = \dfrac{\varepsilon_t}{\sqrt{h_t}}$ and $E(z_t) = \left(\dfrac{2}{\pi}\right)^{1/2}$

The major advantage in using the EGARCH model is that the conditional variance will always be positive no matter what values the parameters take. There is therefore no need for non-negativity constraints on the parameters. This greatly simplifies the estimation process and avoids many of the difficulties normally encountered in the estimation of GARCH models. However, in order to ensure stationarity in the process, the only restriction that is needed in an EGARCH model is that the sum of the β_i terms must not exceed unity.

In the EGARCH model, ε_{t-i}^2 in the GARCH model is effectively substituted by the function $f(z_{t-i})$. This function is the one that enables the model to capture the asymmetric impact of news on volatility. For negative values of ϕ, the term ϕz_t produces asymmetric effects in the model. Furthermore, the term $\gamma\left[|z_t| - E(|z_t|)\right]$ represents a size effect. Residuals that are larger in size than expected have a positive effect on the conditional variance (Nicholls and Tonuri, 1995, p. 381). Notice that in the EGARCH model, the residuals are standardised with respect to current volatility. This provides the model with an additional advantage as this feature allows it to capture extremely large residuals rather than just the moderately-sized ones. During periods of high volatility, large residuals are not uncommon.

In the case of the simple EGARCH(1,1) model, the model is not uniquely identified. Without loss of generality, this problem can be overcome by setting one of the parameters $\{\alpha_1, \phi, \gamma\}$ equal to one. In the later estimation of the parameters of the EGARCH(1,1) model, the parameter γ is set equal to one (Nicholls and Tonuri, 1995, p. 382).

Glosten, Jagannathan and Runkle (GJR) — GARCH Model

Another model that has been proposed to capture such asymmetric effects is Glosten, et al.'s (1993) GJR-GARCH. This model is a simple modification of the linear GARCH framework and is an attractive one to use because there are fewer parameters to estimate in comparison with other asymmetric models of the same order, e.g., EGARCH (p,q) (Nicholls and Tonuri, 1995, p. 383). Engle and Ng (1993) compared the performance of a number of asymmetric volatility models using the Japanese TOPIX stock index returns from 1980 to 1988 and found the GJR-GARCH model to have the best performance. Brailsford and Faff (1993) found the same result with respect to Australian data.

This model expresses the conditional variance in terms of the following (Nicholls and Tonuri, 1995):

$$h_t = \alpha_0 + \sum_{i=1}^{q} \alpha_i \varepsilon_{t-i}^2 \left(1 + \gamma S_{t-i}\right) + \sum_{i=1}^{p} \beta_i h_{t-i}$$

where $S_i = 1$ if $\varepsilon_i < 0$, 0 otherwise.

The GJR-GARCH model is almost similar in structure to the simple GARCH model, except for the inclusion of the factor $\left(1 + \gamma S_{t-i}\right)$ in the second term on the right hand side of the model. The addition of this factor allows the model to capture the asymmetric impact of news on volatility because for "$\gamma < 0$, all negative residuals are weighted and consequently generate a higher level of volatility in subsequent periods than do positive residuals of equal magnitude." (Nicholls and Tonuri, 1995, p. 383)

ARCH-in-Mean (ARCH-M), GARCH-in-Mean (GARCH-M) Model and Other Models

These models which originally came from Engle, et al. (1987) include the conditional variance as an independent variable in their conditional mean equation. Within the finance area, these models are particularly useful in the explanation of returns on financial assets since finance theory states that returns are a function of risk or volatility. However, virtually all studies of stock market volatility, including the Australian study of Brailsford (1992) have found the coefficient of the conditional variance term in the mean equation to be generally insignificant (Nicholls and Tonuri, 1995).

There has been a proliferation of other ARCH-based models which are beyond the scope of this book. The survey article of Bollerslev, et al. (1992) provides a handy reference to these models. As stated earlier, this study limits itself to the use of the GARCH and EGARCH models.

Estimation and Diagnostic Tests

Estimation

The estimation of the parameters of the model entails the following steps.   First, the parameters of the conditional mean equation are estimated and tested.   Then, the residuals from the estimated conditional mean equation are utilised in estimating the parameters of the conditional variance regression.   The parameters of the conditional mean and conditional variance equations can be estimated separately provided the conditional variance term does not appear in the conditional mean equation as this allows the parameters for the two equations to be asymptotically independent (Nicholls and Tonuri, 1995).

Maximum likelihood techniques are commonly used to estimate the parameters of the GARCH(p,q) model.   The Davidson-Fletcher-Powell (DFP) or Berndt, Hall, Hall and Hausman (1974) algorithm (or BHHH for short) may be used.   Bollerslev (1986) discusses how the BHHH algorithm can be applied in the estimation of GARCH parameters.   A fixed lag structure is usually imposed in ARCH and GARCH models in order to avoid problems which may arise from negative volatility estimates (Engle, 1982; and Bollerslev, 1986).

Diagnostics

The primary specification tests for the model involve the Ljung-Box statistic, which is used to test for a lack of serial correlation in the model residuals and in the residuals squared.   This statistic has been shown by McLeod and Li (1983) to be asymptotically chi-square distributed.   The adequacy of the model is checked using the sign bias, the negative size bias, and the positive size bias tests devised by Engle and Ng (1993), as well as the commonly used Ljung-Box test for serial correlation in the squared normalised residuals.   Skewness and kurtosis coefficients for the normalised residuals are also analysed.

Skewness and Kurtosis

The skewness and kurtosis statistics are important diagnostic statistics as they provide an indication as to whether the use of an ARCH-based model is necessary. For a normal distribution, skewness and excess kurtosis estimates are both zero. If the skewness statistic is significantly less than zero (see Taylor, 1986), this would indicate that the data are not symmetric and are in fact negatively — or left-skewed. This characteristic strongly supports the fitting of asymmetric GARCH models to the data. Furthermore, if the kurtosis statistic has a relatively large value, this suggests that the underlying data is leptokurtic, or heavily-tailed and sharply-peaked about the mean when compared with the normal distribution. Since all GARCH-based models also feature this property of leptokurtosis, it would be expected that the use of a GARCH model would at least partially, if not fully, capture the leptokurtosis in the data.

One approach to testing the normality assumption is to use the Jarque and Bera (1980) and Bera and Jarque (1982) or JB test which is actually just a test for skewness and excess kurtosis. The test is based on the following null hypothesis (Davidson and MacKinnon, 1993, p. 568):

$$E\left(u_t^3\right) = 0 \text{ and } E\left(u_t^4\right) = 3\sigma^4$$

For a normal distribution with variance σ^2, the third central moment which determines skewness is zero while the fourth central moment, which determines kurtosis, is $3\sigma^4$. If the third central moment is not zero, the distribution is skewed. If the fourth central moment is larger than $3\sigma^4$, the distribution is said to be leptokurtic, while if the fourth central moment is smaller than $3\sigma^4$, the distribution is said to be platykurtic. In practice, residuals are frequently leptokurtic and rarely platykurtic (Davidson and MacKinnon, 1993, pp. 567-568). The Jarque-Bera statistic is computed as:

$$\left(\frac{T-m}{6}\right)\left(SK^2 + \frac{EK^2}{4}\right)$$

where m = number of regressors, SK is skewness and EK is excess kurtosis. The statistic is distributed as a $\chi^2(2)$.

Ljung-Box (1978) Test

An ARCH-based model implies autocorrelation in the squared errors from the conditional mean equation. The Ljung-Box (1978) statistic provides a test for the presence of autocorrelation in a sample of time series data. LB(k) is the Box-Ljung statistic identifying the presence of first-order autocorrelation in the returns residuals for k lags. Under the null hypothesis of no autocorrelation, it is distributed as $\chi^2(k)$. $LB^2(k)$ is the Box-Ljung portmanteau misspecification test statistic, as suggested by McLeod and Li (1983) identifying the presence of first-order autocorrelation in the squared returns (conditional heteroskedasticity or second moment dependencies). Under the null hypothesis of no autocorrelation, it is distributed as $\chi^2(k)$. If LB^2 is significant, stock market returns exhibit second moment dependencies and should not be modelled as white noise linear processes, e.g., AR or ARMA processes (Nicholls and Tonuri, 1995; Brailsford and Faff, 1993; Longin and Solnik, 1995, p. 12; and Theodossiou and Lee, 1995, p. 293).

If the value of the LB(k) statistic is significant, this indicates that there is evidence for autocorrelation in the stock return series that should be accounted for in the mean equation. Additionally, if the value of the $LB^2(k)$ statistic points to strong autocorrelation in the squares of the stock returns, this result strongly points to volatility clustering. Therefore, in this particular situation, it might be appropriate to use an ARCH-based model to represent the conditional variance of the data. If the model appropriately captures the ARCH effects, then the LB statistic of the squared normalised residuals should not be significant (Nicholls and Tonuri, 1995; and Brailsford and Faff, 1993).

Lagrange Multiplier Test

The appropriateness of an ARCH-based model can also be tested using the Lagrange multiplier (LM) test presented in Engle (1982). The test for a univariate ARCH process involves estimating the mean equation with OLS and regressing the squared residuals from the OLS regression on constant and q lagged values of themselves. If T is the number of observations and R^2 is the coefficient of determination, from the auxiliary regression, then $T.R^2 \sim \chi^2_q$ is the test statistic for the null hypothesis of no ARCH against the alternative hypothesis of ARCH(q) (Kroner and Sultan, 1991, p. 404).

The LM test statistic is asymptotically distributed as chi-square with m degrees of freedom when the null hypothesis is true, where m is the number of parameter restrictions. It is asymptotically equivalent to the LR test and hence is also asymptotically the most powerful test (Engle and Ng, 1993, p. 1759). Engle (1982) developed not only the necessary theory to obtain maximum likelihood estimates of an ARCH model, but also showed how to test for the presence of these effects, via LM tests for ARCH (q) errors. He utilised an equation obtained by regressing the squared residual on its last q lags and taking n times the multiple correlation coefficient, where n is the size of the utilised data sample. This statistic follows a $\chi^2(q)$ distribution, where q is the number of degrees of freedom (Alexakis and Apergis, 1996, p. 694).

Engle and Ng (1993) Test of Asymmetry of News Impact

Another set of diagnostic tests for ARCH-based models are the sign bias test, negative size bias test, and the positive size bias test developed by Engle and Ng (1993). "These tests examine whether the squared normalised residual can be predicted by some variables observed in the past which are not included in the volatility model being used. If these variables can predict the squared normalised residual, then the variance model is misspecified. These tests focus on the potential symmetry of the volatility response to past innovations. These tests are conducted jointly in the following OLS regression model:

$$z_t^2 = a + b_1 S_t^- + b_2 S_t^- \varepsilon_{t-1} + b_3 S_t^+ \varepsilon_{t-1} + v_t$$

where z_t are the standardised residuals, S_t^- is a dummy variable that takes a value of unity if ε_{t-1} is negative and zero otherwise and S_t^+ is a dummy variable that takes a value of unity if ε_{t-1} is positive and zero otherwise." (Brailsford and Faff, 1993)

"The sign bias test considers the variable S_t^-, a dummy variable that takes a value of one when ε_{t-1} is negative and zero otherwise. This test examines the impact of positive and negative return shocks on volatility not predicted by the model under consideration. The negative size bias test utilises the variable $S_{t-1}^- \varepsilon_{t-1}$. It focuses on the different effects that large and small negative return shocks have on volatility which is not predicted by the volatility model. The positive size bias test utilises the variable $S^+_{t-1}\varepsilon_{t-1}$, where S^+_{t-1} is defined as $1 - S^-_{t-1}$. It focuses on the different impacts that large and small positive return shocks may have on volatility, which are not explained by the volatility model. Since an important piece of bad news might have a very different impact on volatility than an important piece of good news, it is critical to distinguish between positive and negative return shocks while examining the effects of the magnitude of a piece of news" (Engle and Ng, 1993, pp. 1757 and 1768).

"In the regression model, the sign-bias test relates to the statistical significance or otherwise of the coefficient b_t. If b_t is found to be statistically non-zero, then it indicates that positive and negative innovations impact differently on volatility. The negative (positive) size bias test relates to the statistical significance or otherwise of the coefficient $b_2(b_3)$ in the regression equation. Specifically, if $b_2(b_3)$ is found to be statistically non-zero, then it indicates that large and small negative (positive) innovations impact differently on volatility. The (standard) symmetric GARCH models (the null models) require that b_1, b_2 and b_3 are jointly equal to zero and this joint hypothesis can be tested with the standard F-statistic. Thus, the sign bias, negative bias, and positive bias test statistics are defined as the t-ratios for b_1, b_2 and b_3, respectively, in the regression model while the joint test statistic is represented by the F-statistic on the joint test of b_1, b_2 and b_3" (Engle and Ng, 1993; and Brailsford and Faff, 1993). Engle and Ng (1993) showed how the sign, negative and positive bias tests represent extensions of an LM test statistic and performed Monte Carlo experiments of their finite sample properties.

Previous Studies

The following previous studies show that the equity markets being investigated in this book are characterised by the presence of ARCH effects.

Lee and Ohk (1991) examined the conditional heteroskedasticity of stock return series of Hong Kong, Japan, Korea, Singapore, Taiwan, and the US using an ARCH-M model and daily data from 1981 to 1988. They found strong ARCH effects in all six countries. Chan and Karolyi (1991), using daily Nikkei Stock Average data from 1986 to 1990, found that a GARCH model characterises the Japanese stock market.

Bae and Karolyi (1994), using intraday open and closing prices of the Nikkei Stock Average and Standard and Poor's 500 (S&P 500), investigated the volatility spill-overs between Japan and the US stock markets. Two asymmetric GARCH models, the GJR-GARCH and the PNP-GARCH, were applied to allow for the differing impacts of "bad" news and "good" news. They found that "'bad' news from domestic and foreign markets appear to have a much larger impact on subsequent return volatility than 'good news'. The magnitude and persistence of shocks originating in New York or Tokyo that transmit to the other market are significantly understated if this asymmetric effect is ignored. Diagnostic analysis of the residuals suggests that these parsimonious models perform reasonably well." (Bae and Karolyi, 1994, p. 436)

Clare, et al. (1997) investigated the volatility of the stock market returns of Australia, Hong Kong, Malaysia, Philippines and Singapore based on daily stock market data from 1986 to 1994 and found ARCH effects characterised by GARCH (p,q) models. On the other hand, Hamao, et al. (1990) examined the transmission of the first and second moments in common stock prices across Tokyo, London and New York with the use of daily opening and closing prices of the Nikkei 225 Stock Index, Financial Times-Stock Exchange 100 Share Index, and the Standard and Poor's 500 Composite Index from 1985 to 1988. The analysis was based on a GARCH(1,1)-M model. "Evidence of price volatility spill-overs from New York to Tokyo, London to Tokyo, and New York to London is observed, but no price volatility spill-over effects in other directions are found for the October 1987 period" (Hamao, et al., 1990, p. 281).

Hamao, et al. (1991) again examined the volatility spill-over effects across the US, UK and Japan but this time comparing those of the pre-crash and after-crash periods. They used daily data for the same indices but over the period 1985 to 1990. A GARCH model rather than a GARCH-M model was found to be more appropriate. "They found evidence that volatility spill-over effects emanating from Japan have been gathering strength over time, especially after the 1987 crash."

Using daily returns on the Australian Fifty Leaders Statex — Actuaries Accumulation Index from 1988 to 1991, Nicholls and Tonuri (1995) sought to explain the volatility of the Australian stock market by fitting several asymmetric GARCH models (i.e., EGARCH, AGARCH and GJR-GARCH). The EGARCH(1,1) model was found to best fit the data. Kearns and Pagan (1991) also investigated the monthly volatility of the Australian stock market over the period 1875–87, and fitted ARCH, GARCH and EGARCH models to the data. It was found that the asymmetric EGARCH(1,2) model was the best representation of the volatility of returns.

Theodossiou and Lee (1995) studied the nature of stock market volatility and its relation to expected returns for ten industrialised countries — Australia, Belgium, Canada, France, Italy, Japan, Switzerland, the UK, the US and (West) Germany, using aggregate weekly stock market returns during the period 1976 to 1991. Significant conditional heteroskdasticity is found to be present in the return series of all ten markets, indicating the presence of volatility clustering, that is, the tendency of large stock price changes to be followed by large stock price changes, but with unpredictable sign. A GARCH-M model is used to examine the conditional variance and expected market returns relationship. Stock market volatility in Australia is best represented by a GARCH(1,0) or an ARCH(1) model. Thus, conditional variance of the returns in Australia during a week is influenced only by volatility shocks during the previous week. Stock market volatility in the remaining markets is best represented by low-order GARCH(1,1) process, i.e., is a function of past volatility shocks and past conditional variances from the previous week. Contrary to Australia's situation, volatility shocks in these markets tend to persist for more than one week. No relationship is found between conditional volatility and expected returns in any of the ten national stock markets (Theodossiou and Lee, 1995, pp. 289–290).

Engle and Ng (1993) examined the impact of news on volatility in the Japanese stock market using daily stock market data from 1980 to 1987. Three asymmetric versions of the GARCH(1,1) model were fitted: EGARCH, GJR and PNP. The best model turned out to be the GJR. The EGARCH can also capture most of the asymmetry; however, there is evidence that the variability of the conditional variance is too high. An earlier study by Ng, et al. (1991) investigated stock market volatility spill-overs between Japan, Korea, Taiwan, Thailand and the US using daily data from 1985 to 1987. They found ARCH effects for all the five countries. A GARCH(1,1)-M model was adopted in the analysis.

Koutmos (1996) studied lead/lag and volatility interactions among the stock markets of the UK, France, Germany and Italy with the use of a VAR-EGARCH model. The study found significant lead/lag relationships and asymmetric volatility interactions among the markets. The study, therefore concluded that the European stock markets are integrated. Poon and Taylor (1992) examined the relationship between returns and volatility in the UK stock market during the period 1965 to 1989. GARCH(1,1) and exponential ARCH models were fitted with the use of daily, weekly, fortnightly and monthly data. The GARCH(1,1) model gave the best results. The results however did not establish any clear relationship between returns and volatility. Tse and Tung (1992) also used a GARCH(1,1) model to forecast the volatility of the Singapore stock market during the period 1975 to 1988 based on daily data. They compared this with the volatility forecast derived from two other methods: exponentially weighted moving average (EWMA) and the naive method based on the historical sample variance. The EWMA provided the best results rather than the GARCH method. Table 7.1 presents a summary of these studies.

Empirical Results

As mentioned in the introduction section of this chapter, GARCH and EGARCH models with no cross effects for the conditional variance equation are used in this study. An attempt was made to fit VAR-GARCH and VAR-EGARCH models which allow for cross effects in the conditional variance equations. However, no convergence could be achieved with these models during the iteration process. This is because the full VAR-GARCH or VAR-EGARCH models require the estimation of a large number of coefficients which make the iteration process very long particularly for the parameters in the variance equations. Moreover, the relatively small size of the database (423 observations) made the convergence of the iterative method very difficult especially when some of the coefficients are not strongly significant. As observed by Diebold, (1988) GARCH effects tend to decrease by temporal aggregation as the distribution of returns tends toward normality.

The following conditional mean and conditional variance equations are estimated:

Conditional mean equation: $Y_t^{(i)} = \lambda + \sum_i \mu_i Y_{t-1}^{(i)} + \varepsilon_t$

where i = 1 (Australia), 2 (Japan), 3 (Hong Kong), 4 (Singapore), 5 (US), 6 (UK), 7 (Taiwan), 8 (Korea), 9 (Malaysia), 10 (Indonesia), 11 (Philippines), 12 (Thailand)

Conditional variance equation:

GARCH(1,1) model : $h_t = \alpha_0 + \alpha_1 \varepsilon_{t-1}^2 + \beta_1 h_{t-1}$

EGARCH(1,1) model: $\log h_t = \alpha_0 + \alpha_1 f(z_{t-1}) + \beta_1 \log h_{t-1}$

where $f(z_t) = \phi z_t + \gamma[|z_t| - E(|z_t|)]$, $z_t = \dfrac{\varepsilon_t}{\sqrt{h_t}}$

Table 7.1   Summary of stock market studies using ARCH methodology

Study	Countries	Data	ARCH model
Bae and Koralyi (1994) • asymmetric transmission of volatility across markets • internationalise Engle and Ng (1993) "news impact curve"	US and Japan	Intraday S&P 500 and Nikkei from 1988–92	GARCH: GJR-GARCH and PNP-GARCH
Clare, et al. (1997) • seasonal patterns in volatility	Australia, Hong Kong, Malaysia, Philippines and Singapore	Daily, 1986–94; Australia – All Share Index; Hong Kong – Hang Seng; Malaysia – KL Stock Exchange Composite Index; Philippines – Manila Composite Index; Singapore – Straits Times Index	GARCH(p,q)
Hamao, et al. (1990) • price change and volatility spill-overs	US, Tokyo and London	Daily and intraday Nikkei 225, FTSE 100 and S&P 500, 1985–88	GARCH(1,1)-M
Hamao, et al. (1991) • changes in volatility spill-overs before and after 1987 crash	Tokyo, London and New York	Daily Nikkei 225, FTSE 100 and S&P 500, 1985–90	GARCH (rather than GARCH-M)

Koutmos (1996) • mean and volatility interactions (symmetry) between markets	France, Germany, Italy and UK	Daily, 1986–91 (1562 observations)	Multivariate VAR-EGARCH • asymmetric volatility transmission (higher volatility for bad news than for good news)
Ng, et al. (1991) • extent of transmission of price volatility from US to Pacific markets	US, Tokyo, Korea, Taiwan and Thailand	Daily S&P 500, TOPIX, Korea Composite Stock Price Index, Taiwan Stock Exchange Stock Price Index and SET, 1985–87	GARCH-M
Nicholls and Tonuri (1995) • modelling stock market volatility	Australia	Australian 50 Leaders Statex – Actuaries Accumulation Index daily, 1988–91 (1023 observations)	EGARCH(1,1)
Poon and Taylor (1992) • relationship between returns and volatility in UK context	UK	Daily, weekly, fortnightly and monthly FT All Shares Index, 1965–89	GARCH(1,1), GARCH-M and Exponential ARCH; GARCH(1,1) gave best results
Theodossiou and Lee (1995) • relation between stock market volatility and returns	Australia, Belgium, Canada, France, Italy, Japan, Switzerland, UK, US and West Germany	Weekly aggregate stock market returns, 1976–91 (833 observations)	GARCH-M • ARCH effect present in all markets
Tse and Tung (1992) • forecast volatility for Singapore stock market	Singapore	Daily SES All Share, All finance, All Hotel, All Industrial and Commercial and All Property Indices, 1975–88	GARCH(1,1) model

An EGARCH(1,1) model is used whenever convergence is achieved in the estimation process; otherwise, a GARCH(1,1) model is utilised. Prior evidence from both overseas and Australian markets have shown that a GARCH(1,1) order model provides a reasonable fit for high frequency stock return data. Higher order GARCH formulations are noted to add little to the power of the model and are generally inferior under Akaike's Information Criterion (see Akgiray, 1989; Baillie and DeGennaro, 1990; Schwert and Seguin, 1990; and Brailsford and Faff, 1993). The log-likelihood is maximised using the BHHH (1974) algorithm. All calculations are done with the use of the RATS econometric software.

Note that the conditional mean equation is multivariate and therefore allows for cross effects between markets. The conditional variance equation, however, is univariate and therefore does not provide for spill-over effects of volatility between markets. Since the main focus of the book is on the analysis of interactions between markets, only the conditional mean equation estimates are therefore reported.

Australia and Its Major Trading Partners

This section reports the results of the GARCH and/or EGARCH model analysis of the interaction between the equity markets of Australia and its major trading partners of Japan, Hong Kong, Singapore, US, UK, Taiwan and Korea for three subperiods: before deregulation; before the crash, and after the crash. As previously stated in Chapter 4, the data for Taiwan and Korea are available only during the period after the crash; hence, these two countries are not included in the analyses for the other periods. During the period after the crash, the analysis of the interaction of Taiwan and Korea with Australia is not conducted together with the other markets in one regression equation as doing this leads to non-convergence in the iteration process. Thus, Korea and Taiwan's interaction with the Australian market is separately analysed from the other markets' interaction with Australia during the period after the crash.

Period before Financial Deregulation

Preliminary diagnostics   Table 7.2 presents the results of preliminary diagnostics conducted on the raw returns data for the period before financial deregulation. The skewness statistics presented in row 3

Table 7.2   Preliminary diagnostics for Australia and its major trading partners — period before deregulation (P-values in parentheses)

		Australia (1)	Japan (2)	Hong Kong (3)	Singapore (4)	US (5)	UK (6)
1	Mean	0.0019	0.0028	0.0024	0.0039	0.0017	0.0030
2	Variance	0.0008	0.0004	0.0024	0.0009	0.0004	0.0013
3	Skewness	–0.2240	0.1752	–0.5840	0.7560	0.1366	0.5767
4	Kurtosis	6.2840	3.3058	7.7370	10.0914	4.0297	6.1503
5	Jarque-Bera (JB)	0.0000* (0.0000)	0.0000 (0.1203)	0.0005* (0.0000)	0.0010* (0.0000)	0.0000* (0.0000)	0.0002* (0.0000)
6	LB(12)	29.1997* (0.0037)	27.876* (0.0058)	17.3111 (0.1383)	54.3307* (0.0000)	4.7116 (0.9669)	12.5731 (0.4008)
7	$LB^2(12)$	14.3653 (0.2780)	52.327* (0.0000)	34.9848* (0.0005)	118.716* (0.0000)	37.3128* (0.0002)	158.333* (0.0000)

* significant at the 5 per cent level

indicate that all the time series are skewed with Singapore the most highly skewed and the US the least. Australia and Hong Kong exhibit negative skewness while the other markets show positive skewness. The excess kurtosis statistics shown in row 4 reveal that all of the time series are leptokurtic with Singapore again being the most leptokurtic and Japan the least. The Jarque-Bera (JB) statistics in row 5 indicate that, with the exception of Japan, all stock markets are characterised by non-normalities. The Ljung-Box (LB) portmanteau test statistics on levels, in row 6, show that Australia, Japan and Singapore exhibit linear dependencies. The LB statistics on the squared returns point to nonlinear dependencies in all the time series, except Australia. These nonlinear dependencies most likely are due to ARCH effects (e.g., Nelson, 1991; Akgiray, 1989; Booth et al., 1992; among others). This, therefore, justifies the need to account for ARCH effects in the regression model involving these markets. These results are in line with previous studies (Koutmos, 1992; Nicholls and Tonuri, 1995; Brailsford and Faff, 1993; among others).

Estimation results and residual-based diagnostics   Table 7.3 shows the results of the estimates of the parameter for each stock market in

Table 7.3 Conditional mean interaction between Australia and its trading partners — period before deregulation (P-values in parentheses) (all based on EGARCH Model)

Conditional mean equation: $Y_t^{(i)} = \lambda + \sum_i \mu_i Y_{t-1}^{(i)} + \varepsilon_t$ for $i = 1,2,3,4,5,6$

Conditional variance equation:

EGARCH(1,1) model: $\log h_t = \alpha_0 + \alpha_1 f(z_{t-1}) + \beta_1 \log h_{t-1}$

where $f(z_t) = \phi z_t + \gamma\left[|z_t| - E(|z_t|)\right]$, $z_t = \dfrac{\varepsilon_t}{\sqrt{h_t}}$

Test of asymmetry of news impact:

$$z_t^2 = a + b_1 S_t^- + b_2 S_t^- \varepsilon_{t-1} + b_3 S_t^+ \varepsilon_{t-1} + v_t$$

	Australia (1)	Japan (2)	Hong Kong (3)	Singapore (4)	US (5)	UK (6)
1. Effect on Australia μ_i	0.107 (0.251)	−0.029 (0.632)	0.050[a] (0.046)	−0.024 (0.630)	0.147[a] (0.030)	0.046[b] (0.093)
2. Effect of Australia μ_1	0.107 (0.251)	−0.048 (0.139)	−0.014 (0.185)	−0.021 (0.550)	0.002 (0.955)	−0.058 (0.339)
3. Jarque-Bera (JB)	45.221[a] (0.000)	4.326 (0.115)	192.536[a] (0.000)	540.776[a] (0.000)	12.016[a] (0.002)	0.312 (0.856)
4. LB(12)	0.519 (0.902)	1.287 (0.223)	1.891[a] (0.034)	0.227 (0.997)	0.7448 (0.707)	0.455 (0.940)
5. LB^2(12)	7.035 (0.796)	16.733 (0.116)	22.788[a] (0.019)	1.372 (0.999)	8.982 (0.624)	3.734 (0.978)
6. Sign Test (t-value for b_1)	−1.241 (0.215)	1.166 (0.244)	−0.169 (0.865)	−0.491 (0.624)	−1.335 (0.183)	0.623 (0.533)
7. Negative Test (t-value for b_2)	−0.738 (0.461)	0.698 (0.485)	0.441 (0.659)	−0.347 (0.729)	−0.324 (0.746)	0.425 (0.671)
8. Positive Test (t-value for b_3)	−1.346 (0.179)	0.167 (0.867)	−1.246 (0.213)	−1.198 (0.231)	−1.944[a] (0.052)	−0.067 (0.946)
9. Joint Test (F-value for b_1, b_2 and b_3)	0.801 (0.494)	0.566 (0.638)	0.627 (0.598)	0.566 (0.638)	1.309 (0.271)	0.217 (0.884)

a significant at the 5 per cent level
b significant at the 10 per cent level

the conditional mean equation based on the application of an EGARCH(1,1) model using the data for the period before deregulation. It also shows the different diagnostic statistics on the standardised residuals. The numbers in row 1 (effect on Australia) are the parameter estimates for the Australia regression, i.e., with Australia as the dependent variable. On the other hand, the numbers in row 2 (effect of Australia) are the parameter estimates for Australia as one of the independent variables in the regression for each of the markets (as the dependent variable). The parameter estimates for the other markets as the independent variables in the regression for each market are no longer reported since this section of the book is only concerned with Australia's interaction with other markets and not with the interaction between markets other than Australia.

Rows 3 to 9 in each column are the calculated diagnostic statistics (discussed previously) for the regression equation of each market in columns 1 to 6. Row 3 (JB) statistics indicate whether the regression has been able to account for the non-normalities in the data. A significant JB statistic means the regression equation has not been able to do so. The statistics in rows 4 and 5 indicate whether or not the model captures the nonlinearities in the conditional mean and conditional variance, respectively. Of more importance in this chapter are the nonlinearities in the conditional variance which refer to the ARCH effects. If the statistic is significant, this indicates that the model is not able to capture these nonlinearities. The numbers in rows 6 to 8 for each column are the calculated t-ratios for the parameter estimates of the regression equation used to conduct Engle and Ng's (1993) tests (sign bias, negative bias and positive bias) of asymmetric impact of news on volatility. The statistics shown in row 9 for each column are the calculated F-statistics for the joint tests on b_1, b_2 and b_3. If any of these statistics in rows 6 to 9 is significant, particularly the calculated F-statistic in row 9, then the conditional variance equation is unable to fully capture the asymmetric impact of volatility and, hence, misspecified.

Looking at the numbers in row 1 (effect on Australia), it can be seen that the US, UK and Hong Kong significantly affect Australia while the other markets do not, as shown by their significant P-values. None of the numbers in row 2 (effect of Australia) are significant which means that Australia did not have an influence on any market during the period before deregulation. These results therefore provide further evidence on the influence of the UK and US markets on Australia during the period before deregulation, as earlier found in Chapter 4 of this study. The influence of Australia on Hong Kong, however, is not supported by the results in Table 7.3 — rather, it is Australia that is affected by Hong Kong.

Caution, however, must be exercised in the interpretation of the results arising from the Australian, Hong Kong, Singapore and US regressions (columns 1, 3, 4 and 5). These regressions did not fully capture the non-normalities of the data as shown by the significant JB statistics (row 3) for these markets. The Hong Kong regression (column 3) also did not fully account for the ARCH effect on the data as indicated by its significant LB portmanteau (row 5) statistic. On the other hand, the regression equations for the other markets — Japan and the UK (columns 2 and 6), were able to fully capture the non-normalities, ARCH effect and asymmetric effects of news as shown by the absence of any significant statistic in rows 3, 5 and 9 for these markets. Hence, more confidence can be placed in the results obtained from the Japan and UK regressions.

Period Before the Stock Market Crash

Preliminary diagnostics   As shown in Table 7.4, as with the before financial deregulation data, all of these series are also skewed (row 3) and leptokurtic (row 4) during the period before the crash. Non-normalities characterise the time series for Japan, Hong Kong, Singapore and the US (columns 2, 3, 4 and 5) as indicated by the significant JB statistics (row 5). Australia and the UK (columns 1 and 6), however, did not exhibit any non-normalities as can be seen from their non-significant JB statistics (row 5). None of the markets also had linear dependencies as shown by the absence of any significant statistics in row 6. With the exception of Hong Kong (column 3), all the markets did not show any nonlinear dependencies and ARCH effects as none of the statistics in rows 6 and 7 are significant.

Estimation results and residual-based diagnostics   Table 7.5 presents the estimation results based on the data for the period before the crash. Looking at rows 1 and 2, no number is statistically significant. This implies that there is no significant linkage between Australia and the other markets. Again, this gives additional support to the same earlier finding in Chapter 4. Looking at row 3, it can be seen that only the Australian and UK regressions (columns 1 and 6) captured fully the non-normalities of the data as indicated by their non-significant JB statistics (row 3). All the other markets had significant JB statistics and therefore their regressions did not fully account for the non-normalities in the data. All regressions, however, were able to

Table 7.4 **Preliminary diagnostics for Australia and its major trading partners — period before crash (P-values in parentheses)**

	Australia (1)	Japan (2)	Hong Kong (3)	Singapore (4)	US (5)	UK (6)
1. Mean	0.0040	0.0081	0.0076	0.0000	0.0025	0.0052
2. Variance	0.0009	0.0008	0.0011	0.0009	0.0004	0.0008
3. Skewness	−0.1864	−0.1961	−0.3291	0.2066	−0.7320	−0.3311
4. Kurtosis	2.8837	4.3478	5.0833	4.2768	5.6299	3.1049
5. Jarque-Bera (JB)	1.2517 (0.5348)	16.1730* (0.0003)	39.1820* (0.0000)	14.7825* (0.0006)	74.3654* (0.0000)	3.6889 (0.1581)
6. LB(12)	12.5811 (0.4002)	13.7216 (0.3496)	9.6420 (0.6473)	13.6817 (0.3215)	12.1662 (0.4324)	9.0608 (0.6977)
7. LB^2(12)	7.2438 (0.8411)	13.2489 (0.3512)	21.9618* (0.0380)	14.1749 (0.2897)	6.8967 (0.5023)	11.3133 (0.8644)

* significant at the 5 per cent level

capture any ARCH effects as shown by no LB portmanteau statistics (row 5) that are significant. With the exception of Hong Kong (significant bias test statistic in row 8 of column 3), all regressions also captured the asymmetric characteristic of the data as indicated by the absence of any significant statistics in rows 6 to 9 for the different markets.

Period After the Stock Market Crash

Preliminary diagnostics   Table 7.6 contains the results of the preliminary diagnostics for each of the time series during the period after the crash. Again, all the time series are skewed and leptokurtic as shown by the skewness and kurtosis statistics (rows 3 and 4). The JB statistics (row 5) which are all significant, indicate that, with the exception of Japan (column 2), all the series are characterised by non-normalities. The LB^2(12) statistics on the squared returns (row 7) are not significant for Australia (column 1) and the UK (column 6) but are for the other markets. Hence, Australia and the UK do not exhibit any

Table 7.5   Conditional mean interaction between Australia and its trading partners — period before crash (P-values in parentheses)

Conditional mean equation: $Y_t^{(i)} = \lambda + \sum_i \mu_i Y_{t-1}^{(i)} + \varepsilon_t$ for $i = 1,2,3,4,5,6$

Conditional variance equation:

GARCH(1,1) model: $h_t = \alpha_0 + \alpha_1 \varepsilon_{t-1}^2 + \beta_1 h_{t-1}$

EGARCH(1,1) model: $\log h_t = \alpha_0 + \alpha_1 f(z_{t-1}) + \beta_1 \log h_{t-1}$

where $f(z_t) = \phi z_t + \gamma\left[|z_t| - E(|z_t|)\right]$, $z_t = \dfrac{\varepsilon_t}{\sqrt{h_t}}$

The EGARCH model was used for the Australia, Japan, US and UK regressions while the GARCH model was applied for the Hong Kong and Singapore regressions.

Test of asymmetry of news impact:

$$z_t^2 = a + b_1 S_t^- + b_2 S_t^- \varepsilon_{t-1} + b_3 S_t^+ \varepsilon_{t-1} + v_t$$

	Australia (1)	Japan (2)	Hong Kong (3)	Singapore (4)	US (5)	UK (6)
1. Effect on Australia μ_i	0.1460 (0.102)	0.005 (0.946)	0.081 (0.299)	−0.002 (0.974)	−0.008 (0.946)	−0.040 (0.642)
2. Effect of Australia μ_1	0.1460 (0.102)	−0.053 (0.509)	0.063 (0.418)	0.138 (0.112)	−0.020 (0.691)	0.118 (0.175)
3. Jarque-Bera (JB)	0.611 (0.737)	15.788* (0.000)	10.092* (0.006)	6.693* (0.035)	36.22* (0.000)	2.600 (0.272)
4. LB(12)	0.282 (0.991)	0.460 (0.935)	0.632 (0.812)	0.924 (0.525)	0.417 (0.955)	0.900 (0.549)
5. LB^2(12)	4.1645 (0.991)	6.634 (0.828)	4.759 (0.942)	12.941 (0.297)	5.150 (0.924)	10.888 (0.453)
6. Sign Test (t-value for b_1)	−0.970 (0.331)	0.532 (0.595)	−1.075 (0.284)	0.979 (0.329)	−0.291 (0.772)	−0.344 (0.731)
7. Negative Test (t-value for b_2)	−0.611 (0.542)	0.448 (0.654)	−1.332 (0.185)	1.264 (0.208)	−0.563 (0.574)	0.775 (0.439)
8. Positive Test (t-value for b_3)	−0.184 (0.854)	−0.234 (0.815)	−1.677* (0.095)	0.658 (0.512)	−0.956 (0.340)	−0.391 (0.696)
9. Joint Test (F-value for b_1, b_2 and b_3)	0.375 (0.771)	0.232 (0.874)	1.715 (0.166)	0.680 (0.565)	0.651 (0.584)	0.630 (0.597)

* significant at the 5 per cent level

ARCH effects while the other markets do. But as before, even if markets are shown by the preliminary diagnostics not to exhibit any ARCH effects, GARCH or EGARCH models are still fitted in order to confirm whether these results hold.

Estimation results and residual-based diagnostics Table 7.7 contains the results from the estimation of the conditional mean regression based on the EGARCH(1,1) model for each of the time series based on the data for the period after the crash. It can be seen from the numbers in row 1 that the US (column 5) is the only market that affects Australia as it is the only market with a significant parameter estimate. Australia did not affect any of the other markets as shown by the absence of any significant parameter estimate in row 2. These results again are in line with the findings earlier reported in Chapter 4. As before, they should be taken with caution as all the regressions did not fully capture the non-normalities of the data since all the JB statistics (row 3) are significant for all the regression equations or markets. However, all the regressions were able to fully account for ARCH effects as indicated by the absence of any significant statistics in row 5. All the

Table 7.6   Preliminary diagnostics for Australia and its major trading partners — period after crash (P-values in parentheses)

		Australia (1)	Japan (2)	Hong Kong (3)	Singapore (4)	US (5)	UK (6)
1.	Mean	0.0017	0.0003	0.0035	0.0031	0.0022	0.0015
2.	Variance	0.0006	0.0010	0.0011	0.0006	0.0003	0.0005
3.	Skewness	−0.2620	0.2036	−0.6400	−0.5227	−0.3460	0.4215
4.	Kurtosis	4.8567	4.6161	5.9042	6.7703	4.7318	4.5750
5.	Jarque-Bera (JB)	65.4445* (0.0000)	48.8377 (0.2483)	177.108* (0.0000)	269.158* (0.0000)	61.1556* (0.0005)	56.1110* (0.0065)
6.	LB(12)	10.7135 (0.5536)	20.9591* (0.0510)	16.7638 (0.1587)	14.5589 (0.2665)	21.7224* (0.0408)	17.5132 (0.1313)
7.	$LB^2(12)$	13.6528 (0.3234)	92.7455* (0.0000)	48.6961* (0.0000)	79.5924* (0.0000)	62.2142* (0.0000)	8.6240 (0.7347)

* significant at the 5 per cent level

Table 7.7 Conditional mean interaction between Australia and its trading partners — period after crash (P-values in parentheses) (all based on EGARCH model)

Conditional mean equation: $Y_t^{(i)} = \lambda + \sum_i \mu_i Y_{t-1}^{(i)} + \varepsilon_t$ for $i = 1,2,3,4,5,6$

Conditional variance equation:

EGARCH(1,1) model: $\log h_t = \alpha_0 + \alpha_1 f(z_{t-1}) + \beta_1 \log h_{t-1}$

$$\text{where } f(z_t) = \phi z_t + \gamma\left[|z_t| - E(|z_t|)\right], \quad z_t = \frac{\varepsilon_t}{\sqrt{h_t}}$$

Test of asymmetry of news impact:

$$z_t^2 = a + b_1 S_t^- + b_2 S_t^- \varepsilon_{t-1} + b_3 S_t^+ \varepsilon_{t-1} + v_t$$

	Australia (1)	Japan (2)	Hong Kong (3)	Singapore (4)	US (5)	UK (6)
1. Effect on Australia μ_i	−0.030 (0.601)	−0.004 (0.922)	−0.013 (0.790)	−0.067 (0.330)	0.249[a] (0.001)	0.089 (0.179)
2. Effect of Australia μ_1	−0.030 (0.601)	−0.097 (0.159)	−0.018 (0.769)	0.048 (0.302)	−0.006 (0.832)	−0.023 (0.538)
3. Jarque-Bera (JB)	67.399[a] (0.000)	11.280[a] (0.004)	28.583[a] (0.000)	44.747[a] (0.000)	30.397[a] (0.000)	5.222[b] (0.073)
4. LB(12)	0.688 (0.764)	0.805 (0.646)	13.758 (0.247)	0.525 (0.898)	0.986 (0.461)	1.281 (0.227)
5. LB^2(12)	8.796 (0.641)	10.182 (0.514)	13.758 (0.247)	6.565 (0.833)	12.549 (0.324)	14.035 (0.231)
6. Sign Test (t-value for b_1)	−0.936 (0.350)	−0.665 (0.506)	0.101 (0.920)	−0.242 (0.809)	0.729 (0.466)	0.958 (0.338)
7. Negative Test (t-value for b_2)	−0.167 (0.868)	−0.484 (0.628)	0.994 (0.321)	0.105 (0.916)	−0.496 (0.620)	1.628 (0.104)
8. Positive Test (t-value for b_3)	−0.546 (0.585)	−0.704 (0.482)	−1.212 (0.226)	−1.218 (0.224)	1.939[b] (0.053)	−0.681 (0.496)
9. Joint Test (F-value for b_1, b_2 and b_3)	0.350 (0.789)	0.245 (0.865)	0.891 (0.446)	0.598 (0.616)	1.335 (0.262)	1.141 (0.332)

a significant at the 5 per cent level
b significant at 10 per cent level

regressions were also able to capture the asymmetric impact of news on volatility judging from the absence of any significant statistics in rows 6 to 9, except for the US (column 5) which has a significant number in row 8.

Period After Crash: Australia's Interaction with Taiwan and Korea

Due to technical difficulties in achieving convergence when Taiwan and Korea are added to the regression, the interaction of Australia with Taiwan and Korea during the period after the crash was estimated separately.

Preliminary diagnostics Table 7.8 shows the preliminary diagnostic results for the three time series. Again, each of the time series is skewed and leptokurtic as can be judged from the skewness (row 3) and kurtosis (row 4) statistics, although Taiwan (column 3) exhibits only mild skewness (skewness statistics in row 4 of just −0.0604). The numbers in row 5 indicate that Australia (column 1) and Taiwan (column 3) exhibit non-normalities, as shown by their significant JB statistics, while Korea (column 2) does not (JB statistics not significant). The statistics in row 7 show that Korea and Taiwan have ARCH characteristics (significant statistics) while Australia does not.

Table 7.8 **Preliminary diagnostics for Australia, Taiwan and Korea — period after crash**

	Australia (1)	Korea (2)	Taiwan (3)
1. Mean	0.0014	0.0015	0.0018
2. Variance	0.0006	0.0010	0.0034
3. Skewness	−0.2863	0.2205	−0.0604
4. Kurtosis	4.9545	3.1405	4.9822
5. Jarque-Bera (JB)	71.5532[a]	3.6940	68.0288[a]
	(0.0000)	(0.1577)	(0.0000)
6. LB(12)	12.9383	15.5356	0.0941
	(0.3735)	(0.2134)	(0.1996)
7. $LB^2(12)$	9.1779	19.3332[b]	0.1649[a]
	(0.6877)	(0.0808)	(0.0000)

a significant at 5 per cent level
b significant at 10 per cent level

Estimation results and residual-based diagnostics   The results of the EGARCH(1,1) estimation for each of the time series are shown in Table 7.9. It can be seen from row 1 that Taiwan (column 2) has a significant statistic while Korea (column 3) does not. This means that Taiwan significantly affects Australia while Korea does not. On the other hand, from row 2, it is shown that Australia (column 1) does not have any significant effect on either Taiwan or Korea as indicated by the absence of any significant statistic. The regression model for each of the time series did not capture all the non-normalities in the data as indicated by the JB statistics in row 3 which are all significant. The model for Taiwan and Korea also did not fully account for ARCH effects as indicated by their significant statistics in row 5. All regressions fully captured the asymmetric impact of news as there are no significant sign, negative, positive and joint bias statistics in rows 6 to 9.

Summary

A summary of the results of the analysis of the conditional mean interaction between Australia and its major trading partners is given in Table 7.10. As can be seen in this table, during the period before deregulation, Australia was significantly influenced by the US, UK and Hong Kong but it did not influence any other market. This provides further support to the study's earlier finding that the US and the UK are influential on Australia. During the period before the crash, the ARCH-based analyses confirm the earlier finding that Australia did not have any significant interaction with other markets. Finally, during the period after the crash, the earlier result that the US influences Australia is supported by the results of the ARCH-based analyses. Thus, the analyses in this chapter enables this book to have even greater confidence in its earlier finding that the US and the UK influence the Australian equity market.

ASEAN

This section presents the results of the ARCH-based model analyses on the interaction among the ASEAN equity markets.

Preliminary Diagnostics

Table 7.11 provides the preliminary diagnostic statistics for five ASEAN markets.

Table 7.9 **Conditional mean interaction between Australia and Taiwan and Korea —
period after crash (P-values in parentheses)
(all based on EGARCH model)**

Conditional mean equation: $Y_t^{(i)} = \lambda + \sum_i \mu_i Y_{t-1}^{(i)} + \varepsilon_t$ for $i = 1, 7, 8$

Conditional variance equation:

EGARCH(1,1) model: $\log h_t = \alpha_0 + \alpha_1 f(z_{t-1}) + \beta_1 \log h_{t-1}$

where $f(z_t) = \phi z_t + \gamma \left[|z_t| - E(|z_t|) \right]$, $z_t = \dfrac{\varepsilon_t}{\sqrt{h_t}}$

Test of asymmetry of news impact:

$z_t^2 = a + b_1 S_t^- + b_2 S_t^- \varepsilon_{t-1} + b_3 S_t^+ \varepsilon_{t-1} + v_t$

		Australia (1)	Taiwan (2)	Korea (3)
1.	Effect on Australia μ_i	0.000 (0.999)	−0.013[a] (0.021)	0.015 (0.665)
2.	Effect of Australia μ_1	0.000 (0.999)	0.036 (0.692)	0.026 (0.686)
3.	Jarque-Bera (JB)	28.521[a] (0.000)	5.864[a] (0.053)	4.650[b] (0.098)
4.	LB(12)	0.514 (0.906)	2.372[b] (0.006)	1.449 (0.141)
5.	LB^2(12)	6.332 (0.850)	28.949[b] (0.002)	18.598[b] (0.069)
6.	Sign Test (t-value for b_1)	0.071 (0.944)	0.689 (0.491)	−0.146 (0.884)
7.	Negative Test (t-value for b_2)	0.071 (0.944)	−0.098 (0.922)	−0.022 (0.982)
8.	Positive Test (t-value for b_3)	−1.037 (0.300)	−0.493 (0.622)	−0.101 (0.919)
9.	Joint Test (F-value for b_1, b_2 and b_3)	0.478 (0.698)	0.781 (0.505)	0.009 (0.999)

a significant at 5 per cent level
b significant at 10 per cent level

Table 7.10 Summary of conditional mean interaction between the equity markets of Australia and its major trading partners

Period	Japan	Hong Kong	Singapore	Taiwan	Korea	US	UK
Before Deregulation							
Effect on Australia	NS	S	NS	NS	NS	S	S
Effect of Australia	NS	NS	NS	NS	NS	NS	NS
Before Crash							
Effect on Australia	NS	NS	NS	NS	NS	NS	NS
Effect of Australia	NS	NS	NS	NS	NS	NS	NS
After Crash							
Effect on Australia	NS	NS	NS	NS	NS	S	NS
Effect of Australia	NS	NS	NS	NS	NS	NS	NS

S = significant
NS = not significant

Table 7.11 Preliminary diagnostics for ASEAN

	Malaysia (1)	Singapore (2)	Indonesia (3)	Thailand (4)	Philippines (5)
1. Mean	0.0029	0.0030	0.0039	0.0040	0.0035
2. Variance	0.0009	0.0006	0.0023	0.0017	0.0014
3. Skewness	−0.4731	−0.5387	3.6879	−0.5636	−0.2148
4. Kurtosis	4.6188	6.8307	37.2042	12.4037	4.8207
5. Jarque-Bera (JB)	0.00001[a] (0.0000)	0.0000[a] (0.0000)	0.0002[a] (0.0000)	0.0002[a] (0.0000)	0.0000 (0.7772)
6. LB(12)	20.5230[b] (0.0578)	19.0026[b] (0.0885)	38.8605[a] (0.0001)	19.4012[b] (0.0793)	27.9635[a] (0.0056)
7. LB^2(12)	78.7350[a] (0.0000)	124.9786[a] (0.0000)	8.1023 (0.7771)	124.9786[a] (0.0000)	52.2572[a] (0.0000)

a significant at 5 per cent level
b significant at 10 per cent level

Again, all markets are skewed (row 3) and leptokurtic (row 4). All the JB statistics (row 5) are significant and this confirms the existence of non-normalities in the markets. All markets exhibit nonlinearities in their conditional mean as shown by row 6 statistics which are all significant. Furthermore, with the exception of Indonesia (column 3), all markets exhibit ARCH effects as indicated by the significant statistics in row 7.

Empirical Results and Residual-based Diagnostics

The results of the regression estimation based on the ASEAN data are presented in Table 7.12. No results are available for Indonesia (column 3) due to non-convergence in the estimation process. The results here show that it is Thailand rather than Malaysia that is the dominant market in ASEAN as shown by Thailand's (row 4) significant parameter estimates in relation to all the markets. Only Thailand had a significant linkage with each market as indicated by the absence of any other significant parameter estimate for the other markets (rows 1, 2, 3 and 5).

Again, caution must be exercised in accepting these results. The Thailand regression (column 4) was able to capture the non-normalities of the data, as shown by its JB statistic (row 6) which was not significant, but was unable to fully account for the ARCH effects as indicated by its significant statistic in row 8. The regressions for the other markets (columns 1, 2 and 5) did not capture the non-normalities in the data as can be seen from their significant JB statistics (row 6) but were able to fully account for the ARCH effects as indicated by their non-significant statistics in row 8. All regressions captured the asymmetric effects of news on volatility as no statistics was significant in rows 9 to 12.

Australia and the ASEAN

This section presents the results of the ARCH-based model analyses on the interaction between the Australian and ASEAN equity markets.

Preliminary Diagnostics

From the previous discussion, it has already been established that the Australian and ASEAN time series are all skewed and leptokurtic with the ASEAN markets exhibiting ARCH effects.

Table 7.12　Conditional mean interaction among the ASEAN

Conditional mean equation:

$$Y_t^{(i)} = \lambda + \sum \mu_i Y_{t-1}^{(i)} + \varepsilon_t \text{ for } i = 4,9,10,11,12$$

Conditional variance equation:

GARCH(1,1) model: $h_t = \alpha_0 + \alpha_1 \varepsilon_{t-1}^2 + \beta_1 h_{t-1}$

EGARCH(1,1) model: $\log h_t = \alpha_0 + \alpha_1 f(z_{t-1}) + \beta_1 \log h_{t-1}$

where $f(z_t) = \phi z_t + \gamma \left[|z_t| - E(|z_t|) \right]$, $z_t = \dfrac{\varepsilon_t}{\sqrt{h_t}}$

The EGARCH model was used for the Malaysia, Singapore and Philippines regressions while the GARCH model was applied for the Thailand regression.

Test of asymmetry of news impact:

$$z_t^2 = a + b_1 S_t^- + b_2 S_t^- \varepsilon_{t-1} + b_3 S_t^+ \varepsilon_{t-1} + v_t$$

Explanatory markets	Markets explained				
	Malaysia	Singapore	Indonesia[a]	Thailand	Philippines
	(1)	(2)	(3)	(4)	(5)
1. Malaysia	0.081	0.074	–	–0.112	–0.052
	(0.339)	(0.221)		(0.269)	(0.591)
2. Singapore	0.020	–0.002	–	0.144	0.185
	(0.856)	(0.978)		(0.296)	(0.107)
3. Indonesia	0.006	0.001	–	0.009	0.015
	(0.825)	(0.973)		(0.740)	(0.712)
4. Thailand	0.087[b]	0.065[b]	–	0.203[b]	0.141[c]
	(0.021)	(0.020)		(0.001)	(0.009)
5. Philippines	–0.012	0.014	–	0.079	0.123[b]
	(0.778)	(0.677)		(0.134)	(0.044)
6. Jarque-Bera (JB)	13.675[b]	44.219[b]	–	37.952	28.432[b]
	(0.001)	(0.000)		(0.000)	(0.000)
7. LB(12)	0.499	0.4587	–	1.674[b]	0.759
	(0.915)	(0.938)		(0.070)	(0.693)
8. $LB^2(12)$	5.813	6.040	–	19.518[b]	9.812
	(0.886)	(0.871)		(0.052)	(0.547)
9. Sign Test (t-value for b_1)	–1.511	–0.784	–	–1.595	–0.325
	(0.132)	(0.434)		(0.111)	(0.745)
10. Negative Test (t-value for b_2)	–1.170	–0.201	–	–1.577	0.298
	(0.243)	(0.841)		(0.116)	(0.766)
11. Positive Test (t-value for b_3)	–1.391	–1.588	–	–0.855	–0.283
	(0.165)	(0.113)		(0.393)	(0.777)
12. Joint Test (F-value for b_1, b_2 and b_3)	1.116	0.878	–	1.186	0.126
	(0.342)	(0.452)		(0.315)	(0.945)

a no convergence was achieved
b significant at 5 per cent level
c significant at 10 per cent level

Empirical Results and Residual-based Diagnostics

Table 7.13 shows the estimation results based on the EGARCH(1,1) model as applied to the data for Australia and ASEAN. Earlier in this study, it has been found that Australia is significantly affected by Malaysia, Singapore and Thailand but not vice versa. This finding does not obtain further support from the results presented in Table 7.13. As can be seen in row 1 of this table where no statistic is significant, Australia is not affected by any of the ASEAN markets and, further, as shown by its significant parameter estimate in row 2 of column 3, it is even influential on Singapore. All the regressions failed to capture non-normalities in the data as indicated by the JB statistics (row 3) which are all significant. However, all were able to account for the ARCH effects and asymmetries as can be seen from the absence of any significant statistics in rows 5 to 9.

Summary and Conclusion

This chapter re-examined the short-term linkages among the markets taking into account ARCH effects which are well-recognised in the literature as a feature of stock market data. The results of the diagnostic statistics indicate the presence of non-normalities, asymmetries and ARCH effects in the data and therefore points to the necessity of using a model that takes into account ARCH effects. Either a GARCH(1,1) or EGARCH(1,1) model is used but whenever convergence is achieved, the EGARCH(1,1) model is utilised as this takes into account any asymmetry characteristics in the data. The results obtained in this chapter further support the study's earlier results in Chapter 4 that the US and UK are influential on the Australian market, thus, these findings can be accepted with even greater confidence. It should be noted that the findings in this chapter are based on univariate rather than multivariate VAR ARCH-based models due to the difficulty in achieving convergence in the estimation process for the latter models. Hence, even if any earlier finding does not find further support from the results in this chapter, this earlier finding remains acceptable pending further investigation based on multivariate VAR ARCH-based models in the future.

Table 7.13　Conditional mean interaction between Australia and the ASEAN (P-values in parentheses) (all based on EGARCH model)

Conditional mean equation:

$$Y_t^{(i)} = \lambda + \sum_i \mu_i Y_{t-1}^{(i)} + \varepsilon_t \text{ for } i = 1,4,9,10,11,12$$

Conditional variance equation:

$$\text{EGARCH(1,1) model: } \log h_t = \alpha_0 + \alpha_1 f\left(z_{t-1}\right) + \beta_1 \log h_{t-1}$$

$$\text{where } f\left(z_t\right) = \phi z_t + \gamma\left[\left|z_t\right| - E\left(\left|z_t\right|\right)\right], \ z_t = \frac{\varepsilon_t}{\sqrt{h_t}}$$

Test of asymmetry of news impact:

$$z_t^2 = a + b_1 S_t^- + b_2 S_t^- \varepsilon_{t-1} + b_3 S_t^+ \varepsilon_{t-1} + v_t$$

	Australia (1)	Malaysia (2)	Singapore (3)	Indonesia (4)	Philippines (5)	Thailand (6)
1. Effect on Australia μ_i	−0.0347 (0.478)	0.026 (0.760)	−0.032 (0.765)	−0.004 (0.861)	−0.128 (0.700)	0.017 (0.650)
2. Effect of Australia μ_1	−0.0347 (0.478)	0.074 (0.134)	0.085[b] (0.029)	a	0.042 (0.570)	−0.074 (0.295)
3. Jarque-Bera (JB)	58.156[b] (0.000)	11.223[b] (0.004)	41.922[b] (0.000)	a	26.916[b] (0.000)	23.716[b] (0.000)
4. LB(12)	0.769 (0.683)	0.496 (0.917)	0.437 (0.948)	a	0.762 (0.6895)	1.1037 (0.355)
5. $LB^2(12)$	8.459 (0.672)	5.848 (0.883)	5.7145 (0.892)	a	9.840 (0.545)	13.208 (0.280)
6. Sign Test (t-value for b_1)	−0.939 (0.348)	−1.312 (0.190)	0.728 (0.467)	a	0.469 (0.639)	−1.502 (0.134)
7. Negative Test (t-value for b_2)	−0.863 (0.389)	−0.961 (0.337)	0.493 (0.622)	a	0.647 (0.518)	−1.296 (0.196)
8. Positive Test (t-value for b_3)	−0.535 (0.593)	−1.286 (0.199)	−0.736 (0.462)	a	0.130 (0.897)	−0.516 (0.606)
9. Joint Test (F-value for b_1, b_2 and b_3)	0.373 (0.773)	0.869 (0.457)	0.822 (0.482)	a	0.152 (0.929)	0.896 (0.443)

a no value as no convergence was achieved
b significant at 5 per cent level

8 Summary of Results, Implications and Conclusion

Aims and Methodology

The book investigates equity markets integration among three groups of countries in the Asia-Pacific region: (a) Australia and its major trading partners (Japan, Hong Kong, Singapore, Taiwan, US and UK), (b) ASEAN (Malaysia, Singapore, Indonesia and Philippines) and (c) Australia and the ASEAN. Integration is operationally defined to be price interdependence, following Kenen (1976) in order to avoid the difficulties pointed out by Shepherd (1994) when integration is defined in terms of asset substitutability and capital mobility. For each of the three cases, the study aims to answer the following questions:

(a) To what extent are equity prices in these markets significantly linked, both in the short-term and in the long-term?
(b) Which markets lead and which ones lag?
(c) How fast and for how long do interactions occur between these markets?

The extent and structure of interdependence among markets is examined in the short-term as well as in the long-term through the application of recently developed time series econometrics techniques, cointegration, Granger-causality, impulse response, forecast variance decomposition and ARCH model-based analyses, which are, as mentioned earlier, performed within a VAR context — a nonstructural econometric modelling approach. Due to the many difficulties encountered in formulating and applying a rigorous theory to capture the multitude of factors that govern the behaviour of stock market prices, a non-structural rather than a structural modelling approach is more suited to the study of stock market relationships.

The analysis of the interaction between equity markets is conducted in the following sequence. A cointegration test is conducted first since the results from this test serve as inputs to the conduct of the Granger-causality, variance decomposition and impulse response analyses. If cointegration is found, then the latter three must be done, based on error-correction models (ECM). On the other hand, if no cointegration is found, then the analyses is to be based on the regression of the first differences of the variables using a standard VAR model. However, before cointegration can be done, the variables have to be tested for stationarity and optimum lags have to be determined Finally, the ARCH model-based analysis is conducted in order to check whether the results obtained from the other techniques are supported or rejected when ARCH effects are considered.

Unit root tests are performed to determine whether each data series is stationary (unit roots do not exist). To do this, both the augmented Dickey-Fuller or ADF for short (Said and Dickey, 1984) and the Phillips-Perron (1988) or PP for short tests are conducted. On the other hand, the likelihood ratio test is conducted to determine the optimum number of lags to be used in the VAR models.

Cointegration analysis in time series econometrics, introduced in the mid 1980s, has been regarded by many econometricians as the most important recent development in empirical modelling (Charemza and Deadman, 1992, p. 116). Cointegration analyses can indicate reliably whether there is a long-term equilibrium relationship between the Australian and Asian equity market indices. On the other hand, the error-correction models (ECM) which are derived from cointegration, show how this equilibrium relationship is achieved. Cointegration therefore shows the long-term relationship while the ECM indicates the short-term dynamics in the movement towards long-term equilibrium. Cointegration is performed using the Johansen (1988) and Johansen and Juselius (1990) multivariate maximum likelihood procedure which provides for the determination of the maximum number of cointegrating vector. This procedure has been shown to have certain distinct advantages over other procedures, e.g., Engle and Granger (1987); and Engle and Yoo (1987).

Granger-causality analysis pinpoints the direction of interaction between equity markets in the short-run. The Granger-causality analysis is performed based on the standard VAR model, if the variables are not cointegrated, and on an error-correction model (ECM) if the variables are cointegrated. The ECM captures a new channel of causality which cannot be captured by non-ECM models (Lin and Swanson, 1993). The forecast variance decomposition and impulse response, which are readily available within VAR, measure the duration and speed of interaction between equity markets in the short-run. The analyses are based on the orthogonalised moving average representation of the VAR model derived by the Cholesky decomposition in Eun and Shim (1989). Finally, ARCH-based models are utilised to investigate the short-term interaction between markets taking into account the clustering of volatility that is well-recognised to characterise stock market data. The analysis is conducted based on the GARCH and EGARCH models. The GARCH model assumes a symmetric impact of news on volatility while the EGARCH model allows for asymmetric impact.

As stated earlier, all these techniques are applied with the use of weekly Morgan Stanley Capital International (MSCI) data covering the period 1975–95.

Summary of Results

Equity Market Interdependence Between Australia and Its Major Trading Partners

The book first investigates the equity market price interdependence between Australia and its major trading partners. The investigation is conducted during three subperiods: before financial deregulation (1975–83), before the stock market crash (1984–88) and after the crash (1988–95). In terms of cointegration, it is expected that Australia will not be cointegrated with the other markets during the period before financial deregulation but will be cointegrated with the other markets during the period after deregulation both before the stock market crash and after the crash. Previous research has shown that markets were not linked to other markets before financial deregulation but have become so after deregulation. An example is the case of Thailand, as found by Ng, et al (1991), and the UK, as discovered by Taylor and Tonks (1989). It has also been shown that markets became more integrated after the crash. This has been the experience of Japan and the US (Campbell and Hamao, 1992; Malliaris and Urrutia, 1992).

In terms of Granger-causality and forecast variance decomposition analyses, it is expected that the Australian market will be influenced by the US and the UK, in line with existing evidence (Eun and Shim, 1989; and McNelis, 1993), but will not have any causal relation with Korea and Taiwan, as these markets are still heavily regulated. These markets have been found not to be linked to other markets by Ng, et al. (1991), Cheung and Mak (1992). The impulse response analysis is expected to show that most of the interaction between Australia and these markets should occur within a period of one week. Previous studies (Malliaris and Urrutia, 1992; Eun and Shim, 1989; and Espitia and Santamaria,

1994) have found that the international transmission of information between markets is completed within a period of two days.

The cointegration test results show that the Australian equity market is not significantly linked with any other equity market in the long-run.   On the other hand, the Granger-causality and forecast variance decomposition analyses revealed that Australia has significant linkages with the US, the UK and Hong Kong over the short-run. This confirms the results of previous studies (Eun and Shim, 1989; Kwan, et al., 1996; and McNelis, 1993). The impulse response analyses showed that the interaction between Australia and these markets occur mostly within a period of four weeks.   Australia's short-term linkage with the US and the UK is supported further by the results from the ARCH-based analyses.

The Australian equity market is therefore linked to the US in the short-run but not in the long-run. This could imply that the Australian equity market overreacts to movements of past prices in the US but this overreaction is corrected over the long-run. The study shows that the US is influential on Australia but Japan is not. This could be interpreted as evidence supporting the claim that the US market is influential worldwide but Japan is not, even at the regional level (Eun and Shim, 1989; Espitia and Santamaria, 1994; Cheung and Mak, 1992). The lack of cointegration between the equity markets of Australia and the US, UK, Hong Kong, Singapore, Taiwan and Korea means that the latter markets could serve as good avenues for long-term portfolio diversification by Australian investors.   In the short-term, Australian investors can reap portfolio diversification benefits from using the markets of Japan, Singapore, Taiwan and Korea.

Equity Market Price Interdependence among ASEAN

The second group of equity markets to be analysed in the book is ASEAN comprising the countries of Malaysia, Singapore, Indonesia, Philippines and Thailand. The analysis is conducted over the period 1988–95. Because of the economic linkage between these countries and the openness of their economies to foreign capital flows as a result of the significant financial deregulation that they have gone through, it is expected that these markets will significantly affect each other. Malaysia and Singapore, being the larger markets, are expected to be influential on the other markets.

The full empirical results in relation to the analysis of the equity market interaction among ASEAN are presented in Chapter 5.   No cointegration was found among the markets as a group. Thus, there is no significant long-term price linkage among the ASEAN equity markets. In the short-term, the results of the Granger-causality test reveal, however, that these markets are all significantly linked with each other. There is a bidirectional causality between: Malaysia and Singapore; Singapore and Thailand; and Malaysia and Thailand. On the other hand, a unidirectional causality occurs between the Philippines and Singapore with causality running from the former to the latter. The forecast variance decomposition analyses show that Malaysia is the most, and Indonesia is the least influential among the ASEAN markets. The results of the impulse response analyses indicate that the interaction among the ASEAN markets occurs immediately and continues even beyond two months. These results, however, could not find further support from those of the ARCH-based analyses. Thus, there is no significant long-term linkage among the ASEAN markets and therefore, these markets can serve as good avenues for long-term portfolio diversification for investors within the ASEAN markets. In the short-term, given the limitations of the ARCH-based analyses, it can still be said that the ASEAN markets are significantly linked and therefore do not provide diversification benefits to short-term investors within ASEAN. Further research on this issue using multivariate ARCH-based models would be more illuminating.

Equity Market Price Linkage Between Australia and ASEAN

The last group of equity markets whose price interaction is investigated in the book is Australia and ASEAN. The analysis is conducted over the period 1988–95. Given the significant trade interaction between Australia and ASEAN since 1980 (DFAT, 1992b) and the significant financial deregulation which has occurred in each of these markets, it is expected that Australia will be cointegrated with ASEAN. Given also that Malaysia and Singapore are the dominant stock markets in ASEAN, it is expected that Australia will be significantly linked to them. Because these markets lie within the same time zone, it is also expected that Australia will respond immediately to any shocks coming from ASEAN within a week's time and ASEAN is expected to do the same with regards to shocks coming from Australia.

The cointegration test finds that Australia is significantly linked with ASEAN in the long-run. The Granger-causality, forecast variance decomposition and impulse response analyses show that in the short-run, Australia is significantly affected by Malaysia, Singapore and Thailand. Australia responds to a Malaysian and Singaporean shock immediately in week 1 and continues its response until week 10. The Australian market is not significantly linked with the Philippines and Indonesia in the short-term. Thus, it can be said ASEAN does not provide portfolio diversification benefits to long-term Australian investors. However, in the short-term, although the ARCH-based analyses did not provide further support, the Philippines and Indonesian markets do.

Implications and Conclusion

In summary, in the case of Australia and its major trading partners, the book finds that Australia is not significantly linked with any other market in the long-term and is only significantly linked with the US and the UK in the short-term. The US and the UK lead Australia. Australia responds to a shock coming from these markets within a week and continues to do so for a period of four weeks. For the ASEAN markets, the book finds no significant linkage among these markets in the long-term. However, in the short-term, with the exception of Indonesia, all these markets have significant linkages with each other with Malaysia being the most influential. Each of these markets responds to a shock from another market within a period of one week but the interaction continues beyond two months. Finally, in the case of Australia's interaction with ASEAN, the study finds that Australia is significantly linked with ASEAN in the long-term and is significantly influenced by Malaysia, Singapore and Thailand in the short-term. Australia responds to a shock from these markets within a week and the interaction continues until week 10.

In terms of implications, these results confirm the finding in the existing literature on equity market integration that markets are either interdependent or segmented, depending on the markets, period and methodology chosen. From the viewpoint of portfolio diversification, these findings also imply that Australia can obtain diversification benefits from (a) its major trading partners in the long-term, (b) Japan, Philippines and Indonesia in the short-term and (c) Taiwan and Korea in both the short-term and long-term. The ASEAN markets also offer diversification benefits to long-term investors within the ASEAN region. The results of the book also imply the existence of inefficiency[1] in the international transmission of news between Australia and the other markets and among the ASEAN markets. This offers possible arbitrage opportunities if appropriate trading strategies can be devised. Furthermore, the findings of the book clearly show that the US and the UK markets are influential but the Australian and Japanese markets are not. This is in line with the findings of Eun and Shim (1989) and Cheung and Mak (1992). Finally, the results of the book also lend further support to the existing evidence that Taiwan and

Korea (Fung and Lie, 1990) and Indonesia (Palac-McMiken, 1997) are markets that do not have significant linkage with other markets.

The finding that Australia is significantly linked with the ASEAN markets should be important for Australian financial and economic regulators particularly in the light of the current Asian financial crisis which is creating worldwide concern. This finding adds weight to the fear of the Asian financial crisis spilling over to Australia and thus provides support to those who argue that Australia should play a more active role in searching for solutions to this crisis. Since the Australian market has been found to be influenced by the US and UK markets, it is also important that Australian financial regulators continue to monitor events occurring in these two markets and explore the possibility of coordinating its financial and economic policies with those in these markets.

This book has analysed the interaction of the three groups of markets also with the use of models allowing for autoregressive conditional heteroskedasticity (ARCH) effects. However, due to problems in achieving convergence and the great amount of computer time that is needed, the book only made use of models that allow for cross-market effects in the mean equations. For further research, it is therefore useful to continue to explore the use of VAR-GARCH type models which also provide for cross-market effects in the conditional variance equations. Also, in terms of future research, it would be highly illuminating if the factors affecting the extent of integration between markets can be identified whereby a model can be constructed that will describe the behaviour of integration between markets over time. In this regard, an index of integration can be constructed which can then be used to test this structural model of integration. Finally a study of financial market integration at a more disaggregated level, e.g., between industries would also be useful in complementing existing results based on market level data.

Note

1   It is generally accepted within the finance literature that efficiency connotes an interaction period of less than a week (see Eun and Shim, 1989, for instance).

Bibliography

Aburachis, A.T. (1993), 'International Financial Markets Integration: An Overview', in S. Stansell (ed.), *International Financial Market Integration*, Blackwell, Cambridge, MA, pp. 26–41.

Aderhold, R., Cumming, C. and Harwood, A. (1988), 'International Linkages Among Equities Markets and the October 1987 Market Break', *Quarterly Review*, Federal Reserve Bank of New York, vol. 13, Summer, pp. 34–46.

Adler, M. and Dumasm, B. (1983), 'International Portfolio Choice and Corporation Finance: A Synthesis', *Journal of Finance*, vol. 38, pp. 925–84.

Agenor, P.R. and Taylor, M.P. (1993), 'The Causality Between Official Parallel Exchange Rates in Developing Countries', *Applied Financial Economics*, vol. 3, pp. 255–66.

Aggarwal, R. and Soenen, L.A. (1989), 'Diversification Benefits of Investing in the Asia-Pacific Region', in E. Kaynak and K.H. Lee (eds), *Global Business: Asia-Pacific Dimensions*, Routledge, London and New York, pp. 335–49.

Aggarwal, R., Mohanty, S. and Song, F. (1996), 'Are Survey Forecasts of Macroeconomic Variables Rational?', *Journal of Business*, vol. 68, no. 1, pp. 99–119.

Agmon, T. (1972), 'The Relations Among Equity Markets: A Study of Share Price Co-Movements in the United States, United Kingdom, Germany and Japan', *Journal of Finance*, vol. 4, pp. 839–1317.

Aitken, M. (1990), 'The Australian Securities Industry Under Negotiated Brokerage Commissions: Evidence of the Effects of Change on the Structure of the Industry', *Journal of Business Finance and Accounting*, vol. 17, no. 2.

Akdogan, H. (1995), The Integration of International Capital Markets: Theory and Empirical Evidence, Edward Elgar, England.

Akgiray, V. (1989), 'Conditional Heteroskedasticity in Time Series of Stock Returns: Evidence and Forecasts', *Journal of Business*, vol. 62, no. 1, pp. 55–80.

Aksu, C. and Gunay, E. (1995), 'An Empirical Analysis of the Causal Relationship Between Short Interest and Stock Prices', *Journal of Business Finance and Accounting*, vol. 22, no. 5, pp. 733–49.

Alexakis, P. and Apergis, N. (1996), 'ARCH Effects and Cointegration: Is the Foreign Exchange Market Efficient?', *Journal of Banking and Finance*, vol. 20, no. 4, pp. 687–97.

Alford, A. (1993), 'Assessing Capital Market Integration: A Review of the Literature', in S. Stansell (ed.), International Financial Market Integration, Blackwell, Cambridge, MA.

Allen, D.E. and Macdonald, G. (1995), 'The Long-run Gains from International Equity Diversification: Australian Evidence from Cointegration Tests', *Applied Financial Economics*, vol. 5, pp. 33–42.

Allen, M. (1991), *The Times Guide to International Finance: How the World Money System Works*, Times Books, UK.

Alogoskoufis, G. and Smith, R. (1995), 'On Error Correction Models: Specification, Interpretation, Estimation', in L. Oxley, D.A.R. George, C.J. Roberts and S. Sayer (eds), *Surveys in Econometrics*, Blackwell, Oxford, UK and Cambridge, USA.

Amelung, T. (1992), 'Regionalization of Trade in the Asia-Pacific: A Statistical Approach', *ASEAN Economic Bulletin*, vol. 9, no. 2, pp. 133–48.

Ammer, J. and Mei, J. (1996), 'Measuring International Economic Linkages with Stock Market Data', *Journal of Finance*, LI, vol. 5, pp. 1743–63.

Ang, J.S. (1991), 'Agenda for Research in Pacific-Basin Finance', in S.G. Rhee and R.P. Chang (eds), *Pacific Basin Capital Markets Research*, Vol. II, Elsevier Science Publishers, Holland.

Antsong, L. and Swanson, P.E. (1993), 'Measuring Global Money Market Interrelationships: An Investigation of Five Major World Currencies', *Journal of Banking and Finance*, vol. 17, pp. 609–28.

Areepong, B. and Stansell, S. (1990), 'A Study of International Financial Market Integration: An Examination of the US, Hong Kong and Singapore Markets', *Journal of Business Finance and Accounting*, vol. 17, no. 2, Spring.

Ariff, M. (1996), 'Effects of Financial Liberalization on Four Southeast Asian Financial Markets, 1973–94', *ASEAN Economic Bulletin*, vol. 12, no. 3, pp. 325–337.

Ariff, M. and Chye, T.E. (1992), 'ASEAN-Pacific Trade Relations', *ASEAN Economic Bulletin*, vol. 8, no. 3, pp. 258–83.

Arshanapalli, B. and Doukas, J. (1993), 'International Stock Market Linkages: Evidence from the Pre- and Post-October 1987 Period', *Journal of Banking and Finance*, vol. 17, pp. 193–208.

Arshanapalli, B. and Doukas, J. (1994), 'Common Stochastic Trends in a System of Eurocurrency Rates', *Journal of Banking and Finance*, vol. 18, no. 6, pp. 1047–61.

Australian Stock Exchange, *Monthly Index Analysis*, 31 May 1994, no. 171.

Ayling, D.E. (1986), *The Internationalisation of Stock Markets*, Gower, England, Chapters 1, 2 and 9.

Bae, K.H. and Karolyi, G.A. (1994), 'Good News, Bad News, and International Spillovers of Stock Return and Volatility Between Japan and the US', *Pacific-Basin Journal of Finance*, vol. 2, pp. 405–38.

Bahmani-Oskooee, M. and Sohrabian, A. (1992), 'Stock Prices and the Effective Exchange Rate of the Dollar', *Applied Economics*, vol. 24, pp. 459–64.

Bailey, W. and Stulz, R. (1990), 'Benefits of International Diversification: The Case of Pacific Basin Stock Markets', *Journal of Portfolio Management*, Summer, pp. 57–61.

Baillie, R.T. and DeGennaro, R.P. (1990), 'Stock Returns and Volatility', *Journal of Financial and Quantitative Analysis*, vol. 25, pp. 203–14.

Baillie, R.T. and Bollerslev, T. (1989), 'The Message in Daily Exchange Rates: A Conditional Variance Tale', *Journal of Business and Economic Statistics*, vol. 7, pp. 297–305.

Baulant, C. and Boutiller, M. (1992), 'Foreign Position in French Francs: An Econometric Study with Data Over the EMS Period', *Economic Modelling*, July, pp. 290–300.

Becker, K., Finnerty, J. and Gupta, M. (1990), 'The Intertemporal Relation Between the US and Japanese Stock Markets', *Journal of Finance*, vol. 45, no. 4, 1297–306.

Bencivenga, V., Smith, B. and Starr, R. (1995), 'Equity Markets, Transaction Costs, and Capital Accumulation: An Illustration', *Conference on Stock Markets, Corporate Finance and Economic Growth*, World Bank Research Committee.

Bennett, P. and Kelleher, J. (1987), 'The International Transmission of Stock Price Disruption in October 1987', *Federal Reserve Bank of New York Quarterly Review*, vol. 13, Summer, pp. 34–46.

Ben-zion, U., Choi, J.J. and Hauser, S. (1996), 'The Price Link Linkages Between Country Funds and National Stock Markets: Evidence from Cointegration and Causality Tests of Germany, Japan and UK Funds', *Journal of Business Finance and Accounting*, vol. 23, no. 7, pp. 1005–17.

Bera, A.K. and Jarque, C.M. (1982), 'Model Specification Tests: A Simultaneous Approach ', *Journal of Econometrics*, vol. 20, pp. 59–82.

Berndt, E.K., Hall, H.B., Hall, R.E. and Hausman, J.A. (1974), 'Estimation and Inference in Nonlinear Structural Models', *Annals of Economic and Social Management*, vol. 4, pp. 653–66.

Black, F. (1972), 'Capital Market Equilibrium with Restricted Borrowing', *Journal of Business*, vol. 45, pp. 444–54.

Black, F. (1974), 'International Capital Market Equilibrium with Investment Barriers', *Journal of Financial Economics*, vol. 1, pp. 337–52.

Black, F. (1976), 'Studies in Stock Price Volatility Changes', *Proceedings of the 1976 Business Meeting of the Business and Economics Statistics Section*, American Statistical Association, pp. 177–81.

Bloch, Ernest (1989), *Inside Investment Banking*, Dow Jones-Irwin, Illinois, pp. 342–362.

Bodman, P.M. (1996), *On Export-Led Growth in Australia and Canada: Cointegration, Causality and Structural Stability*, Discussion Paper No. 200, Department of Economics, University of Queensland, Brisbane, Australia.

Bollerslev, T. (1986), 'Generalised Autoregressive Conditional Heteroskedasticity', *Journal of Econometrics*, vol. 31, pp. 307–27.

Bollerslev, T. (1990), 'Modelling the Coherence in Short-Run Nominal Exchange Rates: A Multivariate Generalised ARCH Model', *The Review of Economics and Statistics*, vol. 72, pp. 498–505.

Bollerslev, T. and Wooldridge, J. (1992), 'Quasi-Maximum Likelihood Estimation and Inference in Dynamic Models with Time-Varying Covariances', *Econometric Reviews*, vol. 11, pp. 143–72.

Bollerslev, T., Chou, R. and Kroner, K. (1992), 'ARCH Modeling in Finance: A Review of Theory and Empirical Evidence', *Journal of Econometrics*, vol. 52, pp. 5–59.

Bonser-Neal, C., Brauer, G., Neal, R. and Wheatley, S. (1990), 'International Investment Restrictions and Closed-End Country Fund Prices', *Journal of Finance*, vol. XLV, no. 2, June, pp. 523–47.

Booth, G.G., Hatem, J., Vitranen, I. and Yli-Olli, P. (1992), 'Stochastic Modeling of Security Returns: Evidence from the Helsinki Stock Exchange', *European Journal of Operational Research*, vol. 56, pp. 98–106.

Bos, T. and Fetherston, T.A. (1995), 'Asian Capital Markets Gaining Recognition and Maturity', in T. Bos and T.A. Fetherston (eds), *Research in International Business and Finance — Rising Asian Capital Markets: Empirical Studies*, Volume 10, JAI Press, Greenwich, Connecticut, USA.

Box, G.E.P. and Pierce, D.A. (1970), 'Distribution of Residual Autocorrelations in Autroregressive Integrated Moving Average Time Series Models', *Journal of the American Statistical Association*, vol. 65, pp. 1590–26.

Brailsford, T.J. (1992), 'The Risk Premium and Exogenous Shifts of Risk in the Australian Equity Market', *Faculty of Economics and Commerce Seminar Series*, Australian National University, Canberra.

Brailsford, T. and Heaney, R. (1998), *Investments: Concepts and Applications in Australia*, Harcourt Brace, Sydney.

Brailsford, T.J. and Faff, R. (1993), 'Modelling Australian Stock Market Volatility', *Australian Journal of Management*, vol. 18, no. 2, pp. 109–32.

Brancato, C.K. (1991), 'The Pivotal Role of Institutional Investors in Capital Markets', in A. Sametz (ed.), *Instituttional Investing: Challenges and Responsibilities of the 21st Century*, Business One Irwin, Illinois.

Brocato, J. (1994), 'Evidence on Adjustments in Major National Stock Market Linkages Over the 1980s', *Journal of Business Finance and Accounting*, vol. 21, no. 5, pp. 643–67.

Brooks, R.D., Faff, R.W. and Lee, J.H.H. (1992), 'The Form of Time Variation of Systemic Risk: Some Australian Evidence', *Applied Financial Economics*, vol. 2, pp. 191–98.

Calvo, S. and Reinhart, C. (1996), 'Capital Flows to Latin America: Is There Evidence of Contagion?', in G. Calvo, M. Goldstein and E. Hochreiter (eds),

Private Capital Flows to Emerging Economies After the Mexican Crisis, Institute for International Economics, Washington D.C.

Campbell, J.Y. and Hentschel, L. (1992), 'No News is Good News: An Asymmetric Model of Changing Volatility in Stock Returns', *Journal of Financial Economics*, vol. 31, no. 3, June, pp. 281–318.

Campbell, J.Y. and Hamao, Y. (1992), 'Predictable Stock Returns in the United States and Japan: A Study of Long-Term Capital Market Integration', *Journal of Finance*, vol. 47, no. 1, pp. 43–69.

Campbell, J.Y., Lo, A.W. and McKinlay, A.C. (1997), *The Econometrics of Financial Markets*, Princeton University Press, New Jersey.

Cargill, T., Cheng, H. and Hutchison, M.M. (1986), 'Financial Market Changes and Regulatory Reforms in Pacific Basin Countries: An Overview', in Hang-Sheng Cheng (ed.), *Financial Policy and Reform in the Pacific Basin Countries*, Lexington Books, Mass.

Chan, K.C. and Karolyi, A. (1991), 'The Volatility of the Japanese Stock Market: Evidence from 1977 to 1990', in W.T. Ziemba, W. Bailey and Y. Hamao (eds), *Japanese Financial Markets Research*, Elsevier Science Publishers.

Chan, K.C. and Lai, P. (1993), 'Unit Root and Cointegration Tests of World Stock Prices', in S.R. Stansell (ed.), *International Financial Market Integration*, Blackwell, Oxford, UK and Cambridge, US.

Chan, K.C., Gup, B.E. and Pan, M.S. (1997), 'International Stock Market Efficiency and Integration: A Study of Eighteen Nations', *Journal of Business Finance and Accounting*, vol. 24, no. 6, pp. 803–13.

Chang, R.P., Kang, J.K. and Rhee, S.G. (1993), *The Behavior of Malaysian Stock Prices*, Working Paper No. WP9302, PACAP Research Center, College of Business Administration, University of Rhode Island.

Charemza, W.W. and Deadman, D.F. (1992), *New Directions in Econometric Practice*, Edward Elgar, UK.

Chaudhuri, K. (1997), 'Cointegration, Error Correction and Granger Causality: An Application with Latin American Stock Markets', *Applied Economics Letters*, vol. 4, no. 8, pp. 469–71.

Chen, N.F., Roll, R. and Ross, S.A. (1986), 'Economic Forces and the Stock Market', *Journal of Business*, vol. 59, no. 3, pp. 383–403.

Cheung, Y.L. (1993), *Intra-Day Returns and Day-End Effect: Evidence from the Hong Kong Equity Market*, Paper presented at the Fifth PACAP Finance Conference, Kuala Lumpur, Malaysia.

Cheung, Y.L. and Mak, S.C. (1992), 'The International Transmission of Stock Market Fluctuation Between the Developed Markets and the Asian-Pacific Markets', *Applied Financial Economics*, vol. 2, pp. 43–47.

Cheung, Y.L. and Ho, Y.K. (1991), 'The Intertemporal Stability of the Relationships Between the Asian Emerging Equity Markets and the Developed Equity Markets', *Journal of Business, Finance and Accounting*, vol. 18, no. 2, 235–54.

Cheung, Y.W. and Ng, L. (1995), 'Equity Price Variation in Pacific Basin Countries', in T. Bos and T. Fetherston (eds), *Advances in Pacific Basin Financial Markets*, vol. 1, pp. 211–27.

Cheung, Y.W. and Ng, L.K. (1992), 'Stock Price Dynamics and Firm Size: An Empirical Investigation', *Journal of Finance*, vol. 47, pp. 1985–97.

Chiang, A. (1984), Fundamental Methods of Mathematical Economics. 3rd ed. McGraw-Hill.

Chinn, M.D. and Frankel, J.A. (1995), 'Who Drives Real Interest Rates Around the Pacific Rim: The USA or Japan?', *Journal of International Money and Finance*, vol. 14, no. 6, pp. 801–21.

Cho, C, Cheol, E. and Senbet, L. (1986), 'International Arbitrage Pricing Theory: An Empirical Investigation', *Journal of Finance*, vol. 41, 313–29.

Choi, J.J. and Severn, A.K. (1991), 'On the Effects of International Risk, Segmentation and Diversification on the Cost of Equity Capital: A Critical Review and Synthesis', *Journal of Multinational Financial Management*, vol. 1, no. 3, pp. 1–17.

Chopra, N., Lakonishok, J. and Ritter, J.R. (1992), 'Measuring Abnormal Performance: Do Stocks Overreact?', *Journal of Financial Economics*, vol. 31, pp. 235–68.

Chorafas, D. N. (1992), *The Globalisation of Money and Securities Markets: The New Products, Players and Markets*, Probus, Illinois, pp. 180–87.

Christ, C.F. (1993), 'Assessing Applied Econometric Results', *Federal Reserve Bank of St. Louis Review*, March/April, pp. 71–94.

Christie, A.A. (1982), 'The Stochastic Behavior of Common Stock Variances: Value, Leverage and Interest Rate Effects', *Journal of Financial Economics*, vol. 10, pp. 407–32.

Chung, P.J. and Liu, D.J. (1994), 'Common Stochastic Trends in Pacific Rim Stock Markets', *Quarterly Review of Economics and Finance*, vol. 34, no. 3, pp. 241–59.

Clare, A., Garrett, I. and Jones, G. (1997), 'Testing for Seasonal Patterns in Conditional Return Volatility: Evidence from Asia-Pacific Markets', *Applied Financial Economics*, vol. 7, no. 5, pp. 517–23.

Clare, A.D., Maras, M. and Thomas, S.H. (1995), 'The Integration and Efficiency of International Bond Markets', *Journal of Business Finance and Accounting*, vol. 22, no. 2, pp. 313–22.

Clements, M.P. (1989), *The Estimation and Testing of Cointegrating Vectors*, Applied Economics Discussion Paper, No. 79, Institute of Economcis and Statistics, University of Oxford.

Cochran, S.J. and Mansur, I. (1993), 'Expected Returns and Economic Factors: A GARCH Approach', *Applied Financial Economics*, vol. 3, pp. 243–54.

Cole, D. (1995), 'Financial Sector Development in Southeast Asia', in S. Zahid (ed.), *Financial Sector Development in Asia*, Oxford University Press, Oxford and New York.

Cole, D.C. (1988), 'Financial Development in Asia', *Asia-Pacific Economic Literature*, vol. 2, no. 2, September, pp. 26–47.

Conrad, J. and Kaul, G. (1988), 'Time Variation in Expected Returns', *Journal of Business*, vol. 61, pp. 409–25.

Corhay, A. and Rad, A.R. (1994), 'Statistical Properties of Daily Returns: Evidence from European Stock Markets', *Journal of Business Finance and Accounting*, vol. 21, no. 2 (March), pp. 271–82.

Corradi, V., Galeotti, M. and Rovelli, R. (1990), 'A Cointegration Analysis of the Relationship Between Bank Reserves, Deposits and Loans: The Case of Italy', *Journal of Banking and Finance*, vol. 14, pp. 199–214.

Crowder, W.J. (1996), 'A Note on Cointegration and International Capital Market Efficiency: A Reply', *Journal of International Money and Finance*, vol. 15, no. 4, pp. 661–64.

Cuthberson, K. (1996), *Quantitative Financial Economics*, John Wiley & Sons.

Cuthbertson, K., Hall, S.G. and Taylor, M.P. (1992), Applied Econometric Techniques, Harvester Wheatsheaf, Hemel Hemstead.

Cutler, D., Poterba, J.M. and Summers, L.H. (1990), 'Speculative Dynamics and the Role of Feedback Traders', *American Economic Review, Papers and Proceedings*, vol. 80, pp. 63–68.

Czerkawsky, C. (1995), 'Stock Trading, Valuation and Stock Price Correlation Among Tokyo, Singapore and New York Markets', *Papers of the Research Society of Commerce and Economics*, vol. 1, no. 72, pp. 33–48.

Darby, M.R. (1986), 'The Internationalisation of American Banking and Finance: Structure, Risk, and World Interest Rates', *Journal of International Money and Finance*, vol. 5, pp. 403–28.

Darnell, A.C. and Evans, J.L. (1990), *The Limits of Econometrics*, Edward Elgar, UK, Chapters 7 and pp. 133–66.

Davidson, R. and Mackinnon, J.G. (1993), *Estimation and Inference in Econometrics*, Oxford University Press, New York and Oxford.

De Bondt, W.F.M. (1991), 'What Do Economists Know About the Stock Market?', *Journal of Financial Management*, Winter, pp. 84–91.

De Bondt, W.F.M. and Thaler, R. (1985), 'Does the Stock Market Overreact?', *Journal of Finance*, vol. XL, no. 3, pp. 793–808.

De Long, J.B., Shleifer, A., Summers, L.H. and Wladmann, R.J. (1990), 'Positive Feedback Investment Strategies and Destabilising Rational Speculation', *Journal of Finance*, vol. 45, pp. 379–95.

DeJong, F., Kemma, A. and Klock, T. (1992), 'A Contribution of Event Study Methodology with and Application to the Dutch Stock Market', *Journal of Banking and Finance*, vol. 16, pp. 11–36.

Demirguc-Kunt, A. and Levine, R. (1995), 'Stock Markets and Financial Intermediaries', Conference on Stock Markets, Corporate Finance, and Economic Growth, World Bank Research Committee.

Demirguc-Kunt, A. and Maksimovic, V. (1995), 'Stock Market Development and Firm Financing Choices', Conference on Stock Markets, Corporate Finance, and Economic Growth, World Bank Research Committee.

Department of Foreign Affairs and Trade (DFAT) (1992a), *Australia and Northeast Asia in the 1990s: Accelerating Change*, Australian Government Publishing Service, Canberra.

Department of Foreign Affairs and Trade (DFAT) (1992b), *Australia's Business Challenge: South-East Asia in the 1990s*, Australian Government Publishing Service, Canberra.

Dhrymes, P. (1973), 'Restricted and Unrestricted Reduced Forms: Asymptotic Distribution and Relative Efficiency', *Econometrica*, vol. 41, pp. 119–34.

Dickey, D.A. and Fuller, W.A. (1981), 'Likelihood Ratio Statistics for Autoregressive Time Series with a Unit Root', *Econometrica*, vol. 49, pp. 1057–72.

Dickey, D.A., Jansen, D.W. and Thornton, D.L. (1994), 'A Primer on Cointegration with an Application to Money and Income', in B.B. Rao (ed.), *Cointegration for the Applied Economist*, St. Martin's Press, NY.

Diebold, F.X. (1988), *Empirical Modelling of Exchange Rate Dynamics*, Springer Verlag, New York.

Doan, T. (1992 & 1995), *RATS User's Manual, version 4.0*, Estima, Evanston, IL.

Domowitz, I. (1990), 'The Mechanics of Automated Trade Execution Systems', *Journal of Financial Intermediation*, pp. 167–94.

Drake, P.J. (1986), 'The Development of Equity and Bond Markets in the Pacific Region', in A.H.H. Tan (ed.), *Pacific Growth and Financial Interdependence*, Allen & Unwin, Sydney.

Drake, P.J. and Stammer, D.W. (1993), 'The Stock Exchange', in M.K. Lewis and R.H. Wallace, *The Australian Financial System*, Longman Cheshire, South Melbourne.

Drysdale, P. (1988), *International Economic Pluralism: Economic Policy in East Asia and the Pacific*, Allen & Unwin, Sydney, Chapter 7.

Dwyer, G. and Hafer, R. (1988), 'Are National Stock Markets Linked?', *Review, Federal Reserve Bank of St. Louis*, vol. 70, pp. 3–14.

Edwards, R. and Wong, K. (1996), 'Regional Cooperation: ASEAN, AFTA and APEC', in R. Edwards and M. Skully (eds), *ASEAN Business Trade and Development*, Butterworth-Heinemann Australia, Australia.

Eijffinger, S. and Van Rixiel, A. (1992), 'The Japanese Financial System and Monetary Policy: A Descriptive Review', *Japan and the World Economy*, vol. 4, no. 4, pp. 291–309.

Eiteman, D.K., Stonehill, A.I. and Moffett, M.H. (1992), *Multinational Business Finance*, 6th edition, Addison-Wesley, Reading, MA.

Elek, A. (1992), 'Trade Policy Options for the Asia-Pacific Region in the 1990s: The Potential of Open Regionalism', *AEA Papers and Proceedings*, vol. 82, no. 2, May, pp. 74–8.

Enders, W. (1995), *Applied Econometric Time Series*, John Wiley & Sons.

Engel, C. (1996), 'A Note on Cointegration and International Capital Market Efficiency', *Journal of International Money and Finance*, vol. 15, no. 4, pp. 657–60.

Engle, R. (1982), 'Autoregressive Conditional Heteroskedasticity With Estimates of the Variance of U.K. Inflation', *Econometrica*, vol. 52, pp. 267–288.

Engle, R. and Bollerslev, T. (1986), 'Modelling the Persistence of Conditional Variances', *Econometric Review*, vol. 5, pp. 1–50.

Engle, R.F. and Granger, C.W.J. (1987), 'Cointegration and Error Correction: Representation, Estimation, and Testing', *Econometrica*, vol. 55, no. 2, pp. 251–76.

Engle, R.F., Lilien, D.M. and Robins, R.P. (1987), 'Estimating Time Varying Risk Premia in the Term Structure: The ARCH-M Model', *Econometrica*, vol. 55, pp. 391–407.

Engle, R. and Ng, V.K. (1993), 'Measuring and Testing the Impact of News on Volatility', *Journal of Finance*, vol. XLVIII, no. 5, pp. 1749–78.

Engle, R.F. and Yoo, B.S. (1987), 'Forecasting and Testing in Cointegrated Systems', *Journal of Econometrics*, vol. 35, pp. 143–159.

Epstein, R.J. (1987), *A History of Econometrics*, North-Holland, Amsterdam.

Errunza, V. and Losq, E. (1985), 'International Asset Pricing Under Mild Segmentation: Theory and Test', *Journal of Finance*, vol. 40, pp. 105–24.

Espitia, M. and Santamaria, R. (1994), 'International Diversification Among the Capital Markets of the EEC', *Applied Financial Economics*, vol. 4, no. 1, pp. 1–10.

Eun, C.S. and Resnick, B.G. (1984), 'Estimating the Correlation Structure of International Share Prices', *Journal of Finance*, vol. 39, pp. 1311–24.

Eun, C.S. and Janakiramanan, S. (1986), 'A Model of International Asset Pricing with A Constraint on the Foreign Equity Ownership', *Journal of Finance*, vol. 41, pp. 897–914.

Eun, C.S. and Shim, S. (1989), 'International Transmission of Stock Market Movements', *Journal of Financial and Quantitative Analysis*, vol. 24, no. 2, pp. 241–56.

Euromoney (1992), 'Australia', in *Guide to Selected Domestic Bond Markets*, pp. 9–10.

Euromoney (1992), *World Economies Handbook*, p. 146.

Fabozzi, F.J. and Modigliani, F. (1992), *Capital Markets: Institutions and Instruments*, Prentice-Hall, New Jersey.

Faff, R.L., Lee, J.H.H. and Fry, T.R.L. (1992), 'Time Stationarity of Systemic Risk: Some Australian Evidence,' *Journal of Business Finance and Accounting*, vol. 19, pp. 253–270.

Fama, E.F. (1990), 'Stock Returns, Expected Returns, and Real Activity', *Journal of Finance*, vol. 45, pp. 1089–108.

Fama, E. and French, K. (1988), 'Permanent and Temporary Components of Stock Prices', *Journal of Political Economy*, April, pp. 246–73.

Fase, M.M.G. (1981), 'The Linkage of Stock Exchange Markets Between Countries: An Empirical Study of Share Price Co-Movements in Eleven Countries', *Economics Letters*, vol. 7, 363–369.

Finnerty, J. and Schneeweis, T. (1979), 'The Co-Movement of International Asset Returns', *Journal of International Business Studies*, vol. 10, no. 3, 66–78.

Fischer, K. and Palasvirta, A. (1990), 'High Road to a Global Marketplace: The International Transmission of Stock Market Fluctuations', *Financial Review*, vol. 25, 371–94.

Flavin, M.A. (1983), 'Excess Volatility in the Financial Markets: A Reassessment of the Empirical Evidence', *Journal of Political Economy*, vol. 91, no. 6, pp. 929–56.

Frankel, J.A. (1991), 'Is A Yen Bloc Forming in Pacific Asia?', in R. O'Brien (ed.), *Finance and the International Economy: The AMEX Bank Review Prize Essays*, University Press, Oxford.

French, K.R. and Poterba, J.R. (1990), 'Japanese and US Cross-Border Common Stock Investments', *Journal of the Japanese and International Economies*, vol. 4, pp. 476–93.

French, K.R. and Poterba, J.R. (1991), 'Investor Diversification and International Equity Markets', *AEA Papers and Proceedings*, vol. 81, no. 2, May, pp. 223–6.

French, K.R., Schwert, G.W. and Stambaugh, R.F. (1987), 'Expected Stock Returns and Volatility', *Journal of Financial Economics*, vol. 19, pp. 3–29.

Freris, A.F. (1991), *The Financial Markets of Hong Kong*, Routledge, London and New York.

Fry, M. (1995), 'Financial Development in Asia: Some Analytical Issues', *Asian-Pacific Economic Literature*, vol. 9, no. 1, pp. 40–57.

Fuller, R.J. and King, J.L. (1990), 'Is the Stock Market Predictable?', *The Journal of Portfolio Management*, Summer, pp. 29–36.

Fuller, W. (1976), *Introduction to Statistical Time Series*, John Wiley, New York.

Fung, H.G. and Lie, C.J. (1990), 'Stock Market and Economic Activities: A Causal Analysis', in S.G. Rhee and R.P. Chang (eds), *Pacific Basin Capital Markets Research*, Elsevier Science Publishing, Holland, pp. 203–14.

Garnaut, R. (1989), *Australia and the Northeast Asian Ascendancy*, Australian Government Publishing Service, Canberra.

Gennotte, G. and Leland, H. (1990), 'Market Liquidity, Hedging, and Crashes', *The American Economic Review*, vol. 80, no. 5, December, pp. 999–1021.

Geweke, J., Meese, R. and Dent, W. (1983), 'Comparing Alternative Tests of Causality in Temporal Systems: Analytic Results and Experimental Evidence', *Journal of Econometrics*, vol. 21, pp. 161–94.

Ghosh, D.K. and Khaksari, S. (1993), 'International Capital Markets: Integrated or Segmented', in S. Stansell (ed.), *International Financial Market Integration*, Blackwell, Cambridge, MA.

Giles, D. (1991), 'Some Recent Developments in Econometrics: Lessons for Applied Economics', *Supplement to the Economic Record*, pp. 3–19.

Giles, D. (1997), 'Causality Between the Measured and Underground Economies in New Zealand', *Applied Economics Letters*, 1997, no. 4, pp. 63–7.

Gjerde, O. and Saettem, F. (1995), 'Linkages Among European and World Stock Markets', *European Journal of Finance*, vol. I, pp. 165–79.

Glen, J. (1995), 'International Comparison of Stock Trading Practices', Conference on Stock Markets, Corporate Finance, and Economic Growth, World Bank Research Committee.

Glosten, L., Jagannathan, R. and Runkle, D. (1993), 'Seasonal Patterns in the Volatility of Stock Index Excess Returns', *Journal of Finance*, vol. 48, pp. 1779–801.

Goldstein, M. (1998), *The Asian Crisis: Causes, Cures, and Systemic Implications*, Institute for International Economics, Washington D.C.

Goletti, F., Ahmed, R. and Farid, N. (1995), 'Structural Determinants of Market Integration: The Case of Price Markets in Bangladesh', *The Developing Economies*, vol. XXXIII, no. 2, pp. 185–202.

Goodhart, C. (1988), 'The International Transmission of Asset Price Volatility', in *Financial Market Volatility*, Federal Reserve Bank of Kansas City, Kansas City, MO, pp. 79–120.

Granger, C.W.J. (1969), 'Investigating Causal Relation by Econometric Models and Cross-Spectral Methods', *Econometrica*, vol. 37, pp. 424–38.

Granger, C.W.J. (1980), 'Testing for Causality: A Personal Viewpoint', *Journal of Economic Dynamics and Control*, vol. 2, pp. 329–52.

Granger, C.W.J. and Morgenstern, O. (1970), *Predictability of Stock Market Prices*, Heath Lexington Books, Lexington, MA.

Grant, J.L. (1987), 'Stock Return Volatility During the Crash of 1987', *Journal of Portfolio Management*, Winter, pp. 69–71.

Greenwald, B. and Stiglitz, J.E. (1992), 'Information, Finance and Markets: The Architecture of Allocative Mechanisms', *Industrial and Corporate Change*, vol. 1, no. 1, pp. 37–63.

Greenwood, J.G. (1986), 'Financial Liberalisation and Innovation in Seven East Asian Economies', in Y. Suzuki and H. Yomo (eds), *Financial Innovation and Monetary Policy: Asia and the West*, University of Tokyo, Tokyo.

Griffith, W., Hill, R.C. and Judge, G.G. (1993), *Learning and Practicing Econometrics*, John Wiley & Sons, New York.

Grubel, H.G. (1968), 'Internationally Diversified Portfolios: Welfare Gains and Capital Flows', *American Economic Review*, vol. 58, no. 5, pp. 1299–314.

Grubel, H.G. and Fadner, K. (1971), 'The Interdependence of International Equity Markets', *Journal of Finance*, vol. 26, pp. 89–94.

Gujarati, D. (1995), *Basic Econometrics*, 3rd edition, McGraw-Hill.

Gultekin, M.N., Gultekin, N.B. and Penati, A. (1989), 'Capital Controls and International Capital Market Segmentation: The Evidence from the Japanese and American Stock Markets', *Journal of Finance*, vol. 44, pp. 849–70.

Hall, S.G. (1989), 'Maximum Likelihood Estimation of Cointegration Vectors: An Example of the Johansen Procedure', *Oxford Economic Bulletin and Statistics*, vol. 51, no. 2, pp. 213–218.

Hamao, Y., Masulis, R.W. and Ng, V. (1990), 'Correlations in Price Changes and Volatility Across International Stock Markets', *The Review of Financial Studies*, vol. 3, no. 2, pp. 281–307.

Hamao, Y., Masulis, R.W. and Ng, V. (1991), 'The Effect of the 1987 Stock Crash on International Financial Integration', in W.T. Ziemba and Y. Hamao (eds), *Japanese Financial Markets*, Elsevier Science Publisher, Holland, pp. 483–502.

Hamilton, J.D. (1994), *Time Series Analysis*, Princeton University Press, New Jersey.

Harvey, A.C. (1990), *Forecasting Structural and Time Series Models and the Kalman Filter*, Cambridge University Press, Cambridge.

Harvey, A.C. (1997), 'Trends, Cycles and Autoregressions', *The Economc Journal*, vol. 107, pp. 192–201.

Harwood, A. and Takahashi, S. (1996), 'Financing Capital Market Intermediaries in Hong Kong', in H.S. Scott and P.A. Wellongs (eds), *Financing Capital Market Intermediaries in East and Southeast Asia*, Kluwer International.

Heng, T.M. and Low, L. (1996), 'Linkages Among the ASEAN Economies: A Multi-Country Model Analysis', *ASEAN Economic Bulletin*, vol. 13, no. 1, pp. 52–73.

Hietala, P.T. (1989), 'Asset Pricing in Partially Segmented Markets: Evidence from the Finnish Market', *Journal of Finance*, vol. 44, pp. 697–718.

Hillard, J.E. (1979), 'The Relationship Between Equity Indices on World Exchanges', *Journal of Finance*, vol. 34, 1, 103–14.

Holden, D. and Perman, R. (1994), 'Unit Roots and Cointegration for the Economist', in B.B. Rao (ed.), *Cointegration for the Applied Economist*, St. Martin's Press, NY.

Holmes, M.J. (1995), 'The ERM and Monetary Integration in the European Union: An Investigation of Long-run Relationships', *Applied Economics*, vol. 27, pp. 1237–43.

Honeygold, D. (1989), *International Financial Markets*, Woodhead-Faulkner, Cambridge, England.

Huat, T.C. (1982), 'Singapore As An International Financial Centre', in Grub, P.D., Huat, T.C., Kuen-chor, K. and Rott, G.H., *East Asian Dimensions of International Business*, Prentice-Hall, New Jersey, Chapter 4, pp. 29–44.

Hughes, H. (1991), 'Does APEC Make Sense?', *ASEAN Economic Bulletin*, vol. 8, no. 2, pp. 125–36.

Hung, B.W.S. and Cheung, Y.L. (1995), 'Interdependence of Asian Emerging Equity Markets', *Journal of Business Finance and Accounting*, vol. 22, no. 2, pp. 281–8.

Ibbotson, R.C., Karr, R.C. and Robinson, A.W. (1982), 'International Equity and Bond Returns', *Financial Analysts Journal*, vol. 38, pp. 61–83.

In, F. and Menon, J. (1996), 'The Long-Run Relationship Between the Real Exchange Rate and Terms of Trade in OECD Countries', *Applied Economics*, vol. 28, no. 9, pp. 1075–80.

Inoue, Y. (1989), 'Globalisation of Business Finance', *Japanese Economic Studies*, Summer, pp. 41–92.

Isaac, J. (1990), *Japanese Equity Markets*, Euromoney, London, pp. 145–6.

Isimbabi, M.J. (1992), 'Comovements of World Securities Markets, International Portfolio Diversification and Asset Returns: A Survey of Empirical Evidence', in S.J. Khoury, *Recent Developments in International Banking and Finance*, vol. 6, Blackwell, Cambridge, MA.

Izan, H.Y., Jalleh, B.R. and Ong, L.L. (1991), 'International Diversification and Estimation Risk: Australian Evidence', *Australian Journal of Management*, June, vol. 16, no. 1, pp. 73–90.

Jacobs, B.I. and Levy, K.N. (1989), 'The Complexity of the Stock Market: A Web of Interrelated Return Effects', *Journal of Portfolio Management*, Fall, pp. 18–27.

Jaffe, J. and Westerfield, R. (1985), 'Patterns in Japanese Common Stock Returns: Day of the Week and Turn-of-the-Year Effects', *Journal of Financial and Quantitative Analysis*, 20, 261–72.

Janakiramanan, S. and Lamba, A.S. (1997), *An Empirical Examination of Linkages Between Pacific-Basin Stock Markets*, unpublished Conference Paper, Department of Accounting and Finance, University of Melbourne, Victoria, Australia.

Jarque, C.M. and Bera, A.K. (1980), 'Efficient Tests for Normality, Heteroskedasticity and Serial Independence of Regression Residuals', *Economics Letters*, vol. 6, pp. 255–9.

Jeng, Y., Kim, C.W. and Wan-Sulaiman, W.M.H. (1992), 'International Transmission of Stock Market Movements and Korea and Taiwan Fund Prices', in S.G. Rhee and R.P. Chang (eds), *Pacific Basin Capital Markets Research*, Vol. III, Elsevier Science Publishers B.V., Holland, pp. 205–23.

Jeon, B.N. and Von Furstenberg, G.W. (1990), 'Growing International Comovement in Stock Price Indexes', *Quarterly Review of Economics and Business*, vol. 30, no. 3, pp. 15–30.

Johansen, S. (1988), 'Statistical Analysis of Cointegration Vectors', *Journal of Economic Dynamics and Control*, vol. 12, pp. 231–54.

Johansen, S. and Juselius, K. (1990), 'Maximum Likelihood Estimation and Inference on Cointegration — With Applications to the Demand for Money', *Oxford Bulletin of Economics and Statistics*, vol. 52, no. 2, pp. 169–210.

Joong-Woong, K. (1988), "Economic Development and Financial Liberalisation in the Republic of Korea: Policy Reforms and Future Prospects", in Urrutia, Miguel (ed.), *Financial Liberalisation and the Internal Structure of Capital Markets in Asia and Latin America*, UN University, Tokyo.

Jorion, P. (1989), 'Asset Allocation with Hedge and Unhedged Foreign Stocks and Bonds', *Journal of Portfolio Management*, pp. 49–54.

Jorion, P. (1989), 'The Linkages Between National Stock Markets', in R.Z. Aliber (ed.), *The Handbook of International Financial Management*, Dow Jones-Irwin, Illinois.

Jorion, P. and Schwartz, E. (1986), 'Integration vs. Segmentation in the Canadian Stock Market', *Journal of Finance*, vol. 41, pp. 603–14.

Joy, O.M., Panton, D.B., Reilly, F.K. and Stanley, A.M. (1976), 'Co-movements of Major International Equity Markets', The Financial Review, 11, pp. 1–20.

Judge, G.G., Carter Hill, R., Griffiths, W.E., Lutkehpohl, H. and Lee, T.C. (1988), *Introduction to Theory and Practice of Econometrics*, John Wiley & Sons, New York.

Juoro, U. (1993), 'Financial Liberalisation in Indonesia: Interest Rates, Money Market Instruments and Bank Supervision', *ASEAN Economic Bulletin*, vol. 9, no. 3, pp. 323–37.

Karolyi, G.A. (1994), *A Multivariate GARCH Model of International Transmission of Stock Returns and Volatility: The Case of the United States and Canada*, Working Paper, The Ohio State University, forthcoming in *Journal of Business and Economic Statistics*.

Karolyi, G.A. and Stulz, R.M. (1996), 'Why Do Markets Move Together? An Investigation of US-Japan Stock Return Comovements', *Journal of Finance*, vol. LI, no. 3, pp. 951–86.

Kasa, K. (1992), 'Common Stochastic Trends in International Stock Markets', *Journal of Monetary Economics*, vol. 29, no. 1, pp. 95–124.

Kearns, P. and Pagan, A.R. (1993), 'Australian Stock Market Volatility', *The Economic Record*, vol. 69, no. 205, June, pp. 163–78.

Kenen, P.B. (1976), *Capital Mobility and Integration: A Survey*, Princeton Studies in International Finance No. 39, Princeton University.

Khanthavit, A. and Sungkaew, J. (1993), *Measuring Tahiland's Barriers to Investment*, Paper presented at the Fifth PACAP Finance Conference, Kuala Lumpur, Malaysia.

Khoury, S.J., Dodin, B. and Takada, H. (1987), 'Multiple Time Series Analysis of National Stock Markets and Their Structure: Some Implications, in S.J.

Khoury and A. Ghosh (eds), *Recent Developments in International Banking and Finance*, D.C. Heath and Co.

Kim, Y. (1990), 'Purchasing Power Parity in the Long Run: A Cointegration Approach', *Journal of Money, Credit and Banking*, vol. 22, pp. 491–503.

King, M. and Wadwhani, S. (1990), 'Transmission of Volatility Between Stock Markets', *Review of Financial Studies*, vol. 3, no. 1, pp. 5–33.

King, M., Sentana, E. and Wadhwani ,(S. 1994), 'Volatility and Links Between National Stock Markets', *Econometrica*, vol. 62, no. 4, 901–33.

Koch, P.D. and Koch, T.W. (1993), 'Dynamic Relationships Among Daily Levels of National Stock Indexes', in S.R. Stansell (ed.), *International Financial Market Integration*, Blackwell, Oxford, UK and Cambridge, US, pp. 299–328.

Koedijk, K.G. and Mahieu, R.J. (1992), 'Asian-Pacific Real Exchange Rates', Applied Financial Economics, 24, pp. 1255–62.

Koh, B.W. (1992), 'Toward the Most Efficient Operation of the Korean Stock Market', in S.G. Rhee and R.P. Chang (eds), *Pacific Basin Capital Markets Research*, Volume III, Elsevier Science Publishers B.V., Holland.

Korajczyk, R. and Viallet., C. (1989), 'An Empirical Investigation of International Asset Pricing', *Review of Financial Studies*, vol. 2, pp. 553–85.

Korajczyk, R.A. (1995), 'A Measure of Stock Market Integration', Conference on Stock Markets, Corporate Finance, and Economic Growth, World Bank Research Committee.

Kortian, T. and O'Regan, J. (1996), *Australian Financial Market Volatility: An Exploration of Cross-Country and Cross-Market Linkages*, Research Discussion Paper No. 9609, Reserve Bank of Australia, Sydney, Australia.

Koutmos, G. (1992), 'Asymmetric Volatility and Risk Return Tradeoff in Foreign Stock Markets', *Journal of Multinational Financial Management*, vol. 2, no. 2, pp. 27–43.

Koutmos, G. (1996), 'Modeling the Dynamic Interdependence of Major European Stock Markets', *Journal of Business Finance and Accounting*, vol. 23, no. 7, pp. 975–88.

Kreinin, M.E. and Officer, L.H. (1978), 'The Marketing Approach to the Balance of Payments: A Survey', *Princeton Studies in International Finance*, vol. 43, Princeton University, Princeton, N.J.

Krol, R. and Ohanian, L.E. (1990), 'The Impact of Stochastic and Deterministic Trends on Money-Output Causality: A Multi-Country Investigation', *Journal of Econometrics*, vol. 45, pp. 291–308.

Kroner, K.F. and Sultan, J. (1991), 'Exchange Rate Volatility and Time Varying Hedge Ratios', in S.G. Rhee and R.P. Chang (eds), *Pacific Basin Capital Markets Research*, Volume II, Elsevier Science Publishers, Holland.

Kwan, A.C.C., Sim, A.B. and Cotsomitis, J.A. (1995), 'The Causal Relationship Between Equity Indices on World Exchanges', *Applied Economics*, vol. 27, pp. 33–7.

Kwok, R.H.F. (1995), 'Market Integration in the Four Newly Industrialised Economies of Asia', in T. Bos and T.A. Fetherston (eds), *Advances in Pacific Basin Financial Markets*, JAI Press, Volume 1, Greenwich, Conn, pp. 199–209

Lee, I. (1992), 'Stock Market Seasonality: Some Evidence from the Pacific-Basin Countries', *Journal of Business, Finance, and Accounting*, vol. 19, no. 2, 199–210.

Lee, I., Pettit, R.R. and Swankoski, M.V. (1990), 'Daily Return Relationships among Asian Stock Markets', *Journal of Business Finance and Accounting*, vol. 17, no. 2.

Lee, S.B. and Ohk, K.Y. (1991), 'Time-Varying Volatilites and Stock Market Returns: International Evidence', in S.G. Rhee and R.P. Chang (eds), *Pacific Basin Capital Markets Research*, Volume II, Elsevier Science Publishers B.V., Holland, pp. 261–81.

Lee, W. Y. and Sachdeva, K.S. (1977), 'The Role of the Multinational Firm in the Integration of Segmented Capital Markets', *Journal of Finance*, vol. XXXII, no. 2, pp. 479–91.

Lessard, D. (1974), 'World, National, and Industry Factors in Equity Returns', *Journal of Finance*, vol. 29, 379–91.

Leung, I.C.W. (1991), 'Clearing & Settlements Systems in Asia-Pacific Markets and Their Future Developments', A Report of the Stock Exchange of Hong Kong.

Levine, R. and Zervos, S. (1995), 'Policy, Stock Market Development and Long-Run Growth', Conference on Stock Markets, Corporate Finance, and Economic Growth, World Bank Research Committee.

Levy, H. and Lerman, Z. (1988), 'The Benefits of International Diversification in Bonds', *Financial Analysts' Journal*, vol. 44, no. 5, pp. 56–64.

Lin, A. and Swanson, P.E. (1993), 'Measuring Global Money Market Interrelationships: An Investigation of Five Major World Currencies', *Journal of Banking and Finance*, vol. 17, pp. 609–28.

Lin, A. and Swanson, P.E. (1997), 'The U.S. Dollar in Money Markets: A Multivariate Cointegration Analysis', *The Quarterly Review of Economics and Finance*, vol. 37, no. 1, pp. 139–50.

Lin, W.L., Engle, R.F. and Ito, T. (1994), 'Do Bulls and Bears Move Across Borders? Transmission of International Stock Returns and Volatility', *Review of Financial Studies*, vol. 7, pp. 507–38.

Lintner, J. (1965), 'The Valuation of Risky Assets and the Selection of Risky Investments in Stock Portfolios and Capital Budgets', *Review of Economics and Statistics*, vol. 47, pp. 13–37.

Ljung, G.M. and Box, G.E.P. (1978), 'On a Measure of Lack of Fit in Time Series Models', *Biometrika*, vol. 65, pp. 297–303.

Lo, A.W. and MacKinley, A.C. (1988), 'Stock Market Prices Do Not Follow Random Walks', *Review of Financial Studies*, vol. 1, pp. 41–66.

Longin, F. and Solnik, B. (1995), 'Is the Correlation in International Equity Returns Constant: 1960–1990?', *Journal of International Money and Finance*, vol. 14, no. 1, pp. 3–26.

Lutkepohl, H. (1993), *Introduction to Multiple Time Series*, Springer–Verlag, Berlin.

Ma, C.K. (1993), 'Financial Market Integration and Cointegration Tests', in S. Stansell (ed.), *International Financial Market Integration*, Blackwell, Oxford, UK and Cambridge, USA.

MacDonald, R. and Taylor, M.P. (1991), 'Financial Markets Analysis: An Outline', in M.P. Taylor (ed.), *Money and Financial Markets*, Basil Blackwell, MA.

Maddala, G.S. (1992), Introduction to Econometrics, McMillan, New York.

Makridakis, S.G. and Wheelwright, S.C. (1974), 'An Analysis of the Interrelationships Among World Stock Exchanges', *Journal of Business Finance and Accounting*, vol. 1, pp. 195–215.

Maldonado, R. and Saunders, A. (1981), 'International Portfolio Diversification and the Intertemporal Stability of International Stock Market Relationships, 1957–1978', *Financial Management*, vol. 10, 54–63.

Malliaris, A.G. and Urrutia, J.L. (1992), 'The International Crash of October 1987: Causality Tests', *Journal of Financial and Quantitative Analysis*, vol. 27, no. 3, pp. 353–64.

Manning, L.M. and Andrianacos, D. (1993), 'Dollar Movements and Inflation: A Cointegration Analysis', *Applied Economics*, vol. 25, pp. 1483–88.

Markowitz, H. (1959), *Portfolio Selection: Efficient Diversification of Investments*, John Wiley, New York.

Marr, M.W., Trimble, J.L. and Varma, R. (1991), 'On the Integration of International Capital Markets: Evidence from Euorequity Offerings', *Financial Management*, Winter, pp. 11–21.

McCarthy, S. and Wright, A. (1996), 'The Benefits to Shareholders of Diversification Via Multinational Corporations — The Australian Evidence', in D.T. Nguyen (1996), *Queensland, Australia and the Asia Pacific Economy*, Papers from the Third International Conference on Economics in Business and Government held at Griffith University, Brisbane, Australia.

McKenzie, C. and Stutchbury, M. (eds) (1992), *Japanese Financial Markets and the Role of the Yen*, Allen & Unwin, Sydney.

McLeod, A. and Li, W. (1983), 'Diagnostic Checking ARMA Time Series Models Using Squared Residual Autocorrelations', *Journal of Time Series Analysis*, vol. 4, pp. 269–73.

McNelis, P.D. (1993), *The Response of Australian Stock, Foreign Exchange, and Bond Markets to Foreign Asset Returns and Volatilities*, Research Discussion Paper, Economic Research Department, Reserve Bank of Australia.

Meerschwam, D.M. (1991), *Breaking Financial Boundaries: Global Capital, National Deregulation and Financial Service Firms*, Harvard Business School Press, Boston, Chapters 3–6.

Merton, R. (1973), 'An Intertemporal Capital Asset Pricing Model', *Econometrica*, vol. 41, pp. 867–887.

Miller, M.H. (1991), 'Volatility, Episodic Volatility, and Coordinated Circuit-Breakers', in S.G. Rhee and R.P. Chang (eds), *Pacific Basin Capital Markets Research*, Volume II, Elsevier Science Publishers, Holland.

Miller, M.H. (1992), 'Volatility, Episodic Volatility, and Coordinated Circuit-Breakers: The Sequel', in S.G. Rhee and R.P. Chang (eds), *Pacific Basin Capital Markets Research*, Volume III, Elsevier Science Publishers, Holland.

Mills, T. (1996), *The Econometric Modelling of Financial Time Series*, Cambridge University Press, UK.

Moosa, I.A. and Bhatti, R.H. (1996), 'Does Europe Have An Integrated Capital Market? Evidence from Real Interest Parity Tests', *Applied Economics Letters*, vol. 3, pp. 517–20.

Nabeya, S. and Tanaka, K. (1990), 'Limiting Power of Unit Root Tests in Time Series Analysis', *Journal of Econometrics*, vol. 46, pp. 247–71.

Naughton, T. (1999), 'The Role of Stock Markets in the Asian-Pacific Region', *Asian-Pacific Economic Literature*, vol. 13, no. 1, pp. 22–35.

Nelson, D. (1991), 'Conditional Heteroskedasticity in Asset Returns: A New Approach', *Econometrica*, vol. 59, pp. 347–70.

Newey, W. and West, K. (1987), 'A Simple, Positive Semi-Definite, Heteroskedasticity and Autocorrelation Consistent Covariance Matrix', *Econometrica*, vol. 55, pp. 703–708.

Ng, V., Chang, R.P. and Chou, R.W. (1991), 'An Examination of the Behaviour of Pacific Basin Stock Market Volatility', in S.G. Rhee and R.P. Chang (eds), *Pacific Basin Capital Markets Research*, vol. 2, Elsevier Science Publishers, Holland, pp. 245–60.

Nicholls, D. and Tonuri, D. (1995), 'Modelling Stock Market Volatility in Australia', *Journal of Business Finance and Accounting*, vol. 22, no. 3, pp. 377–96.

Norrbin, S.C. (1996), 'Bivariate Cointegration Among European Monetary System Exchange Rates', *Applied Economics*, vol. 28, pp. 1505–13.

O'Brien, R. (1992), *Global Financial Integration: The End of Geography*, Printer Publishers, London,.

OECD (1990), 'Financial Systems and Financial Regulation in Dynamic Asian Economies', *Financial Market Trends*, Organisation for Economic Cooperation and Economic Development, Paris.

Officer, R. (1975), 'Seasonality in Australian Capital Markets: Market Efficiency and Empirical Issues', *Journal of Financial Economics*, June, pp. 29–51.

Officer, R.R. and Finn, F.J. (1991), 'The Stockmarket: Introduction to Market Concepts and Overview of Australian Evidence', in R. Ball, P. Brown, F.J.

Finn and R.R. Officer (eds), *Share Markets and Portfolio Theory*, University of Queensland Press, Brisbane, Australia.

Organisation for Economic Cooperation and Development (1990), *Financial Market Trends*

Osterwald-Lenum, M. (1992), 'A Note with Quantiles of the Asymptotic Distribution of the Maximum Likelihood Cointegration Rank Test Statistics', *Oxford Bulletin of Economics and Statistics*, vol. 54, pp. 461–71.

Pagan, A.R. and Schwert, G.W. (1990), 'Alternative Models for Conditional Stock Volatility', *Journal of Econometrics*, vol. 45, pp. 267–90.

Palac-McMiken, E.D. (1997), 'An Examination of ASEAN Stock Markets: A Cointegration Approach', *ASEAN Economic Bulletin*, vol. 13, no. 3, pp. 299–310.

Panton, D.B., V.P. Lessig and O.M. Joy (1976), 'Co-movement of International Equity Markets: A Taxonomic Approach', *Journal of Financial and Quantitative Analysis*, vol. 11, 415–32.

Park, J. and Fatemi, A.M. (1991), 'The Linkages Between the Equity Markets of Pacific-Basin Countries and those of the US, UK and Japan: A Vector Autoregression Analysis', presented at the Third Annual PACAP Conference held in Seoul, June 3–5.

Park, Y.S. (1982), 'A Comparison of Hong Kong and Singapore as Asian Financial Centres', in P.D. Grub, T.C. Huat, K. Kuen-chor and G.H. Rott, *East Asian Dimensions of International Business*, Prentice-Hall, New Jersey.

Pentecost, E.J. and Holmes, M.J. (1995), 'Changes in the Extent of Financial Integration within the European Community between the 1970s and 1980s', *Applied Economics Letters*, pp. 184–7.

Perman, R. (1991), 'Cointegration: An Introduction to the Literature', *Journal of Economic Studies*, vol. 18, no. 3, pp. 3–30.

Petri, P.A. (1995), 'The Interdependence of Trade and Investment in the Pacific', in E.K.Y. Chen and P. Drysdale (eds), *Corporate Links and Foreign Direct Investment in Asia and the Pacific*, Harper Educational, NSW, Australia.

Philippatos, G.C., Christofi, A. and Christofi, P. (1983), 'The Intertemporal Stability of International Stock Market Relationships: Another View', *Financial Management*, vol. 12, 63–69.

Phillips, P.C.B. and Perron, P. (1988), 'Testing for a Unit Root in Time Series Regression', *Biometrika*, vol. 75, pp. 335–46.

Phillips, P.C.B. and Ouliaris, S. (1990), 'Asymptotic Properties of Residual Based Tests for Cointegration', *Econometrica*, vol. 58, pp. 165–93.

Pindyck, R.S. and Rubinfeld, D.L. (1991), *Econometric Models and Economic Forecasts*, 3rd edition, McGraw-Hill International, New York.

Pindyck, R.S. and Rubinfeld, D.L. (1998), *Econometric Models and Economic Forecasts*, 4th edition, McGraw-Hill International.

Poon, S.H. and Taylor, S.J. (1992), 'Stock Returns and Volatility: An Emprical Study of the UK Stock Market', *Journal of Banking and Finance*, vol. 16, pp. 37–59.

Poskitt, D.S. and Tremayne, A.R. (1981), 'An Approach to Testing Linear Time Series Models', *The Annals of Statistics*, vol. 9, pp. 974–86.

Pringle, J.R.H. (1987), *International Financial Trends in East and Southeast Asia*, Working Paper No. 87/5, National Centre for Development Studies, Australian National University, Canberra.

Rahman, M. and Mustafa, M. (1997), 'Dynamic Linkages and Granger Causality Between Short-Term US Corporate Bond and Stock Markets', *Applied Economics Letters*, vol. 4, no. 2, pp. 89–91.

Rasche, R.H. (1993), 'Monetary Aggregates, Monetary Policy and Economic Activity', *Federal Reserve Bank of St. Louis Review*, March/April, pp. 1–35.

Resnick, B.G. (1989), 'The Globalisation of World Financial Markets', *Business Horizons*, November–December.

Rhee, S. G. (1992), *Securities Markets and Systemic Risks in Dynamic Asian Economies*, Organisation for Economic Co-Operation and Development, Paris.

Rhee, S.G., Chang, R.P. and Ageloff, R. (1990), 'An Overview of Equity Markets in Pacific-Basin Countries', in S.G. Rhee and R.P. Chang (eds), *Pacific Basin Capital Markets Research*, Elsevier Science Publisher, Amsterdam.

Richards, A.J. (1995), 'Comovements in National Stock Markets: Evidence of Predictability, but Not Cointegration', *Journal of Monetary Economics*, vol. 36, no. 3, pp. 631–54.

Ripley, D. (1973), 'Systematic Elements in the Linkage of National Stock Market Indices', *Review of Economics and Statistics*, vol. 55, pp. 356–61.

Roll, R. (1977), A Critique of the Asset Pricing Theory's Tests', *Journal of Financial Economics*, vol. 4, pp. 129–176.

Roll, R. (1989a), 'The International Crash of October 1987', in R. Kamphuis, R. Karmendi and J. Watson (eds), *Black Monday and the Future of Financial Markets*, Irwin, Homewood, IL, pp. 35–70.

Roll, R. (1989b), 'Price Volatility, International Market Links, and Their Implications for Regulatory Policies', *Journal of Financial Services Research*, vol. 3, pp. 211–46.

Roll, R. (1992), 'Industrial Structure and the Comparative Behavior of International Stock Market Indices', *Journal of Finance*, vol. XLVII, no. 1, pp. 3–41.

Ross, S. (1976), 'The Arbitrage Theory of Capital Asset Pricing', *Journal of Economic Theory*, vol. 13, pp. 341–60.

Ross, S. (1989), 'Information and Volatility: The Non-Arbitrage Martingale Approach to Timing and Resolution Irrelevancy', *Journal of Finance*, vol. 44, pp. 1–17.

Rowley, A. (1987), 'Asian Stockmarkets: The Inside Story', *Far Eastern Economic Review*, Hong Kong.

Royama, H. (1988), 'The Expansion of Securitization and the Securities Market in Japan', in *The New Tide of the Japanese Securities Market*, Nikko Research Center, Tokyo, p. 3.

Ryan, B., Scapens, R.W. and Theobald, M. (1992), *Research Method and Methodology in Finance and Accounting*, Academic Press, London.

Said, E.S. and Dickey, D.A. (1984), 'Testing for Unit Roots in Autoregressive-Moving Average Models of Unknown Order', *Biometrika*, vol. 71, pp. 599–607.

Sakakibara, E. (1986), 'The Internationalisation of Tokyo's Financial Markets', in A.H.H. Tan and B. Kapur (eds), *Pacific Growth and Financial Interdependence*, Allen & Unwin, Sydney.

Sato, M. (1992), 'Tokyo Equity Market — Its Development and Policies', in S.G. Rhee and R.P. Chang (eds), *Pacific Basin Capital Markets Research*, vol. III, Elsevier Science Publisher, North Holland.

Scarlett, S. (1990), "Disintermediation, Deregulation, Securitisation and Globalisation of Bond Markets", in Brian Terry (ed.), *International Finance and Investment*, Bankers Books Ltd, London.

Scholes, M. and Williams, J. (1977), 'Estimating Betas from Nonsynchronous Data', *Journal of Financial Economics*, vol. 5, pp. 309–27.

Schollhammer, H. and Sand, O.C. (1987), 'Lead-Lag Relationships Among National Equity Markets: An Empirical Investigation', in S.J. Khoury and A. Ghosh (eds), *Recent Developments in International Banking and Finance*, vol. 1, Cambridge, MA, Lexington, 149–68.

Schwert, G.W. (1989), 'Why Does Stock Market Volatility Change Over Time', *Journal of Finance*, vol. 44, pp. 1115–53.

Schwert, G.W. (1990), 'Stock Volatility and the Crash of 87', *Review of Financial Studies*, vol. 3, pp. 77–102.

Schwert, G.W. and P.J. Seguin (1990), 'Heteroscedasticity in Stock Returns', *Journal of Finance*, vol. 45, pp. 1129–55.

Scott, H.S. and Wellons, P.A. (eds) (1996), *Financing Capital Market Intermediaries in East and Southeast Asia*, Kluwer International, Netherlands.

Sentana, E. and Wadhhwani, S. (1992), 'Feedback Traders and Stock Return Autocorrelations: Evidence from a Century of Daily Data', *The Economic Journal*, vol. 102, pp. 415–25.

Shafie, A.G. (1993), *Stability of International Equity Market Relationship*, Paper presented in the Fifth PACAP Finance Conference, Kuala Lumpur, Malaysia.

Shapiro, A.C. (1992), *Multinational Financial Management*, Allyn and Bacon, Boston, London, Sydney and Toronto.

Sharpe, W. (1964), 'Capital Asset Prices: A Theory of Market Equilibrium Under Conditions of Risk', *Journal of Finance*, vol. 19, pp. 425–42.

Shepherd, W.F. (1994), *International Financial Integration: History, Theory and Applications in OECD Countries*, Avebury, England.

Shiller, R.J., Kon-ya, F. and Tsutsui, Y. (1991), 'Investor Behavior in the October 1987 Stock Market Crash: The Case of Japan', *Journal of the Japanese and International Economies*, vol. 5, pp. 1–13.

Shimamura, T. (1989), 'Japan's Financial System', *Japanese Economic Studies*, Spring, pp. 43–88.

Sims, C.A. (1980), 'Macroeconomics and Reality', *Econometrica*, vol. 48, pp. 1–48.

Smith, K. L., Brocato, J. and Rogers, J.E. (1993), 'Regularities in the Data Between Major Equity Markets: Evidence from Granger Causality Tests', *Applied Financial Economics*, vol. 3, pp. 55–60.

Smith, K. L., Brocato, J. and Rogers, J.E. (1995), 'An Analysis of World Capital Market Return/Risk Ratios: A Test of Global Financial Integration During the 1980–1991 Period', *Managerial Finance*, vol. 21, no. 8, pp. 13–31.

Solnik, B. (1974a), 'An Equilibrium Model of the International Capital Market'. *Journal of Economic Theory*, vol. 8, pp. 500–24.

Solnik, B. (1974b), 'An International Market Model of Security Price Behaviour', *Journal of Financial and Quantitative Analysis*, vol. 9, pp. 537–54.

Solnik, B. (1974c), 'The International Pricing of Risk: An Empirical Investigation of the World Capital Market Structure', *Journal of Finance*, vol. 29, pp. 365–78.

Solnik, B. (1977), 'Testing International Asset Pricing: Some Pessimistic Views', *Journal of Finance*, vol. XXXII, no. 2, pp. 503–12.

Solnik, B. (1983), 'International Arbitrage Pricing Theory', *Journal of Finance*, vol. 38, 449–57.

Solnik, B. (1988), *International Investments*, Addison-Wesley, Reading, MA.

Solnik, B. (1991), 'Pacific Basin Stock Markets and International Diversification', in S.G. Rhee and R.P. Chang (eds), *Pacific Basin Capital Markets Research*, vol. 2, Elsevier Science Publishers, Holland, pp. 309–21.

Stapleton, R.C. and Subrahmanyam, M.G. (1977), 'Market Imperfections, Capital Market Equilibrium and Corporate Finance', *Journal of Finance*, vol. XXXII, no. 2, pp. 307–19.

Stehle, R. (1977), 'An Empirical Test of the Alternative Hypotheses of National International Pricing of Risky Assets', *Journal of Finance*, vol. 32, pp. 493–502.

Stock, J.H. (1984), 'Asymptotic Properties of Least Squares Estimates of Cointegrating Vectors', *Econometrica*, vol. 55, pp. 1035–56.

Stonham, P. (1987), *Global Stock Market Reforms*, Gower Publishing, Vermont, USA.

Studendum, A.H. (1992), *Using Econometrics: A Practical Guide*, Harper Collins, New York.

Stulz, R. (1981), 'A Model of International Asset Pricing', *Journal of Financial Economics*, vol. 9, pp. 383–406.

Stulz, R. (1981), 'On the Effects of Barriers to International Investment', *Journal of Finance*, vol. 36, pp. 923–34.

Summers, L.H. (1986), 'Does the Stock Market Rationally Reflect Fundamental Values?', *Journal of Finance*, vol. XLI, no. 3, July, pp. 591–602.

Suzuki, H. (ed.), (1987), *The Japanese Financial System*, Oxford University Press, Oxford,.

Tan, C.H. (1982), 'Singapore As An International Financial Centre', in P.D. Grub, C.H. Tan, K.C. Kwan and G.H. Rott (1982), *East Asian Dimensions of International Business*, Prentice-Hall, New Jersey.

Tan, C.H. (1982), 'The Asian Dollar Market', in P.D. Grub, C.H. Tan, K.C. Kwan and G.H. Rott (1982), *East Asian Dimensions of International Business*, Prentice-Hall, New Jersey.

Tang, G.Y.N., Mak, S.C. and Choi, D.F.S. (1992), 'The Causal Relationship Between Stock Index Futures and Cash Index Prices in Hong Kong', *Applied Financial Economics*, vol. 2, pp. 187–90.

Tang, M. and Butiong, R.Q. (1994), 'Purchasing Power Parity in Asian Developing Countries: A Co-Integration Test', Report No. 17, Asian Development Bank, Manila.

Tashiro, Y. and Osman, D. (1996), 'Financing Capital Market Intermediaries in Taiwan', in H.S. Scott and P.A. Wellongs (eds), *Financing Capital Market Intermediaries in East and Southeast Asia*, Kluwer International.

Taylor, M.P. and Tonks, I. (1989), 'The Internationalisation of Stock Markets and the Abolition of UK Exchange Controls', *The Review of Economics and Statistics*, vol. 71, pp. 332–36.

Taylor, S.J. (1986), *Modelling Financial Time Series*, John Wiley & Sons.

The Australian, 22 February 1994 and 21 August 1997.

Theodossiou, P. and Lee, U. (1995), 'Relationship between Volatility and Expected Returns Across International Stock Markets', *Journal of Business Finance and Accounting*, vol. 22, no. 2, pp. 289–300.

Thilainathan, R. (1995), 'The ASEAN Financial Sector: A Drag or a Leader?', *ASEAN Economic Bulletin*, vol. 12, no. 1, pp. 1–9.

Titman, S. and Wei, K.C.J. (1993), *Understanding Stock Market Volatility: The Case of Korea and Taiwan*, Paper presented at the Fifth PACAP Finance Conference, Kuala Lumpur, Malaysia.

To, M.C., Assoe, K.G. and Pariente, S. (1994), *The Efficiency of Emerging Stock Markets and Their Relationships with the World's Major Stock Exchanges*, CETAI University of Montreal, Montreal.

Toda, H.Y. and Phillips, P.C.B. (1993), 'Vector Autoregressions and Causality', *Econometrica*, vol. 61, pp. 1367–93.

Tschoegl, A.E. (1993), 'Modeling the Behavior of Japanese Stock Indices', in S. Takagi (ed.), *Japanese Capital Markets: New Developments in Regulations and Institutions*, Blackwell, Cambridge, MA.

Tse, Y.K. (1991), 'Stock Returns Volatility in the Tokyo Stock Exchange', *Japan and the World Economy*, vol. 3, pp. 285–98.

Tse, Y.K. and Tung, S.H. (1992), 'Forecasting Volatility in the Singapore Stock Market', *Asia Pacific Journal of Management*, vol. 9, pp. 1–13.

Tucker, A.L., Madura, J. and Chiang, T.C. (1991), *International Financial Markets*, West Publishing Company, St. Paul, New York, Los Angeles, and San Francisco.

Van Horne, J.C. (1990), 'Changing World and Asian Financial Markets', in S.G. Rhee and R.P. Chang (eds), *Pacific Basin Capital Markets Research*, Elsevier Science Publishers (North-Holland).

Watson, J. and Dickinson, J.P. (1981), 'International Diversification, An Ex Post and Ex Ante Analysis of Possible Benefits', *Australian Journal of Management*, vol. 6, no. 1, pp. 125–34.

Wheatley, S. (1988), 'Some Tests of International Equity Market Integration', *Journal of Financial Economics*, vol. 21, pp. 177–212.

Wheatley, S. (1989), 'A Critique of Latent Variable Tests of Asset Pricing Models', *Journal of Financial Economics*, vol. 23, pp. 325–38.

White, K.J. (1993), *SHAZAM User's Reference Manual*, McGraw-Hill.

Yam, T.K. (1992), 'Emerging Economc and Social Realities in East Asia: Some Implications for Australian Business and Public Policy', *Australian Journal of Management*, vol. 17, no. 1, pp. 67–88.

Yan, L.S. (1986), 'ASEAN: Financial Development and Interdependence', in A.H.H. Tan and B. Kapur (eds), *Pacific Growth and Financial Interdependence*, Allen & Unwin, Sydney, pp. 125–43.

Zervos, S. (1995), 'Industry and Country Components in International Stock Returns', Conference on Stock Markets, Corporate Finance, and Economic Growth, World Bank Research Committee.

For Product Safety Concerns and Information please contact our EU representative GPSR@taylorandfrancis.com Taylor & Francis Verlag GmbH, Kaufingerstraße 24, 80331 München, Germany

T - #0138 - 270225 - C0 - 212/152/10 - PB - 9781138704107 - Gloss Lamination